On Tour With Led Zeppelin

On Tour With

Led Zeppelin

COMPILED BY HOWARD MYLETT

Mitchell Beazley

Concert Log and Concert Analysis by Simon Pallet

Thanks to the following people for their assistance, encouragement and help in the preparation of this book: Andy Adams, Rick Barrett, Mick Bonham and family, Roy Carr, Carl L. Dunn, Robert Ellis, Freda Hyatt, Bob Langley, Dave Lewis, Simon Pallet, Sam Rapallo and Bob Walker

A special thanks to Elizabeth and Anita

Editor: Mike Evans   Designer: Mark Winwood
Production Controller: Michelle Thomas   Picture Research: Emily Hedges

First published in Great Britain in 1993
by Mitchell Beazley, an imprint of
Reed Consumer Books Limited, Michelin House, 81 Fulham Road, London SW3 6RB
and Auckland, Melbourne, Singapore and Toronto

©1993 Reed International Books Limited and IPC Magazines Limited
A Catalogue record for this book is available from the British Library
ISBN 1-85732-315-7

Produced by Mandarin Offset   Printed and bound in China

Contents

Introduction

Led Zeppelin emerged from the demise of the Yardbirds – indeed, for a while they were being referred to as the 'New Yardbirds' – in 1968, a year which heralded a new era in rock music. Sixties pop had evolved, through the psychedelic period of '66-'67 and a second wave of blues bands about to burst on the scene, into the 'underground ' movement of so-called progressive music, a sort of thinking-man's rock which took the music rather more seriously than it was often intended, but on the right occasion this at least meant worthwhile bands and artists got the attention they deserved.

In the forefront of championing this music in Britain – based on a newly-emergent circuit of college venues – was DJ John Peel, and the two leading UK music papers the Melody Maker and New Musical Express. Melody Maker, until the mid Sixties catering more for jazz than pop fans, spearheaded this exposure, while the NME was likewise taking the new sounds seriously as it moved away from its traditionally solid pop approach.

A new school of rock writing evolved , led by Chris Welch, Roy Carr, Nick Kent, Roy Hollingworth, Chris Charlesworth, Charles Shaar Murray and others, all represented in this collection of on-the-road journalism which traces the career of Led Zeppelin as it happened.

It was Chris Welch that guitarist Jimmy Page visited at the Melody Maker offices to report that the Yardbirds had split up and he was forming a new group. Not all the initial coverage of the band was favourable of course, and this reflected teething troubles they recognised themselves, but after a slow start in the UK which contrasted with immediate success in America, they quickly came to be seen – and music press coverage was crucial in this – as the most exciting live act on the contemporary scene.

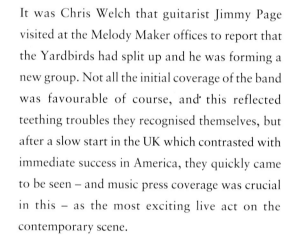

As American audiences fell in love with Zeppelin, the group grew and gelled musically on stage, incorporating their unique form of contemporary blues with lashings of drama, sexuality, tension and showmanship. Each member was contributing fiery elements to the whole, from Jimmy Page's tour-de-force solos to Plant's soaring vocals, with numbers extended to

job to the status of a genre. The picture of life on tour with Zeppelin (both onstage and off) that emerges from these pages, is drawn from the work of Penny Smith, Barry Plummer, Jill Furmanovsky and many more.

As well as becoming musically more ambitious, rock musicians were shown as being verbally articulate for the first time, rather than monosylabic mumblers. Taking the music seriously meant that journalists were taking the musicians seriously too. Hence The Interview. Previously not even the Beatles, who were famous for being both frank and witty when it came to talking to journalists, warranted more than a page or so in a press interview. Now The Interview was a major three or four page feature of the music papers, giving an in-depth insight into a band's attitude to their music, audience, and life generally through the mouths of the stars themselves. The extensive Led Zeppelin interviews herein, therefore, offer a compelling first-person picture of the band at various crucial phases in their dynamic twelve-year career.

the point where set lists looked remarkably short because the performances of each number were becoming so long – but never boring.

Initially Led Zeppelin performances featured sparse stage sets if any at all, with the occasional 'psychedelic' light show flickering in the background, but soon the dramatic quality of their music was matched by spectacular presentation which established the theatrical staging of rock concerts that became the norm in the Seventies and Eighties, especially with the heavy metal bands that Zeppelin helped spawn.

Along with the new breed of music journalists, Melody Maker and NME featured young rock photographers who were to bring a more candid focus to bear on the world of rock'n'roll. No longer was rock photography dominated by the record company press-release studio shot; a gritty realism combined with often highly sophisticated camera techniques lifted what had been a mere

The tragic end to the band came with the untimely death of drummer John Bonham, and only here does the book involve contributions from non-journalists, with short appreciations from fellow percussionists Phil Collins and Cozy Powell, and long-time Led Zeppelin publicist BP Fallon.

My first experience of Led Zeppelin live was in the cavernous but atmospheric environment of Wembley Arena for the 'Electric Magic' concerts of 1971, when they were supported by Stone The Crows and assorted circus acts. I subsequently saw them another six times, and the graphic impressions of those performances and the many more I didn't witness have been brought home in sharp detail while compiling these words and pictures On Tour With Led Zeppelin.

Howard Mylett

Transatlantic Take-Off

Just under a year after their formation in September of 1968, by mid '69 Led Zeppelin had truly been launched on both sides of the Atlantic, causing an immediate sensation in the United States more than in their home base of Great Britain. Their eponymous debut album, made in 30 hours, set the band's tone early in the year with steam-rolling heavy blues that was the forerunner of Heavy Metal, but with the virtuoso touch of Page's brilliant guitar, Plant's soaring vocals and a solid-as-rock rhythm section. It quickly hit the American album Top Ten and paved the way for their first of many treks Stateside. The UK was a slightly slower process, a fact which the band almost resented initially, but the LP got to No.6 boosting a summer tour that culminated in the Bath Blues Festival and the opening night of the Pop Proms at the Albert Hall. A return trip to the States in the Autumn confirmed the band's status as the biggest new thing on the horizon, made plain in November when the follow-up Led Zeppelin II topped the charts at home and in America.

Only Jimmy left to form the new Yardbirds

Chris Welch October 12, 1968

Whatever happened to the Yardbirds? One of the great mysteries of our time; ranking with the Devil's footprints, the Marie Celeste and the Five Penny Post, is the disappearance of a group once hailed as the most progressive in Britain.

When one thinks back, the group that starred Keith Relf and had such distinguished alumni as Eric Clapton, Jeff Beck and Jimmy Page on guitars, were trying experimental

pop long before today's Underground groups.

But unfortunately they were either too early or lacked the drive to carry their breakaway from the original blues formula through to the public.

They found, as have so many British groups, more responsive audiences and better money in the United States of America.

Once they had an enormous following here, but this naturally dwindled with so few appearances and even fewer records. But prior to their departure for the United States they had a period of vacillation.

The departure of Eric, first for a round the world hitchhike (or something), seemed a serious blow to the group. Keith hailed the arrival of Jeff Beck with much excitement, describing him as "The Guv'nor."

Jeff's guitar work had tremendous commercial appeal and numbers like "Jeff's Boogie" raised the group to its highest status and they even started getting hits.

8

Left

Final Yardbirds line-up, 1968

featuring Jimmy Page

Right

Jimmy Page onstage at the

Royal Albert Hall 29/9/69

Below

Band of Joy, 1967

But there were management problems. Paul Samwell-Smith, bass guitarist, left to concentrate on production, never to be heard of again. Jeff got fed up and wanted to quit.

Keith went through a period of infatuation with the music of Bob Lind and released a solo single "Mr Zero."

Nobody quite seemed to know what the Yardbirds were doing. If you asked them, there would be a lot of serious shouting, denials, grumbles and bold future plans announced. Then Jeff left to form his own group.

Now sadly, even Keith Relf, Chris Dreja and Jim McCarty have gone, leaving "new boy" Jimmy Page to form a New Yardbirds.

Good Natured

Jimmy is well-spoken, good-looking and good-natured. He was once one of Britain's youngest session guitarists, his ability to read and feel for modern pop making him much in demand. He gave up the security of the studios to hit the road and play his own solos.

Now Page tells his Yardbird story and describes his new group, which threatens to be a welcome piece of fire power to the armoury of British groups.

"We didn't do any gigs in England for two years, so no wonder we lost popularity. But just before we split we did a couple of colleges that were really fantastic. I was really knocked out."

"We were a happy group and used to get on well socially until we got on stage and Keith lost all enthusiasm. I used to say: 'come on, let's make an effort,' but it had all gone. When they split, I don't think Jim wanted to leave, but Keith was depressed. I think it did us all a favour because the new chaps are only about 19 and full of

Left

Early 1969 USA. Page

playing Paisley

Telecaster, given as

a present by Jeff Beck

Below

Page soon transferred

guitars to trademark

Gibson Les Paul

Opposite

Shepton Mallet, Bath

28/6/69. First UK

outdoor Festival

appearance

enthusiasm. It was getting to be a bit of a trial in the old group."

The line up of Jimmy's new band (and he's not sure whether to call them Yardbirds or not), includes John Paul Jones (organ and bass), Robert Plant (vocals) and Jon Bonham (drums). They made their debut in Denmark.

"It's blues basically, but not Fleetwood Mac style. I hate that phrase progressive blues. It sounds like a hype, but it's more or less what the Yardbirds were playing at the end, but nobody knew about it because they never saw us. We're starting work on an LP and we're going to the States in early November. I'm hoping the Marquee will be a good scene. Robert can get up and sing against anybody. He gets up and sings against Terry Reid! Those two are like brothers together.

"I thought I'd never get a band together. I've always shied of leadership in the past because of all that ego thing. I know old Eric wanted to get a thing together with Stevie but neither of them like leading."

"I didn't want the Yardbirds to break up, but in the end it was too much of a headache. I just wanted to play guitar basically, but Keith always had this thing of being overshadowed by Jeff and that, which was nonsense. It was great when we had the two lead guitars."

Jimmy says all this with a smile and no ill-feeling. And he is far too excited about the future to worry about the past.

"It's refreshing to know that today you can go out and form a group to play the music you like and people will listen. It's what musicians have been waiting for for twenty years".

We're losing too many top groups to America – Zeppelin is latest

by Nick Logan April 5, 1969

Stand up and be counted you British club-goers who arrive at your local hop and head straight for the bar. You Philistines you. It is you who are helping to drive our best musical talents across the Atlantic. And it's a bloody poor show - not to say a downright tragedy.

There's the case of the Cream who played a whole goodbye tour of the States and just two farewell concerts here.

Then there's the news this week that the new Clapton-Baker-Winwood group will probably play just one date in Britain before leaving for a lengthy U.S. tour.

The case to be considered here is that of Led Zeppelin, the group that has now emerged from the old Yardbirds, headed by master guitarist Jimmy Page.

Returning

Having just returned from a sensational debut tour of America, Led Zeppelin is currently playing British club dates before going back to America in mid-April.

We met for lunch and over the melon and Italian nosh the amiable Jimmy sounded off.

"In America the audiences get into their music more. They are more appreciative. They will listen to the sort of patterns you are playing. In Britain all they are interested in is the way to the bar.

"And over there they clap you not because it is the right thing to do. They clap in the right places and it is good because if you are trying to do something and everyone in the audience is spurring you on then it really gets you at it.

"Most places here they just go to have a dance or to have a drink. Not to listen. They don't care who is on.

"Of course there is more money to be made in America but the main reason is that the public is more appreciative."

Jimmy's slamming of the British club-goer isn't a sweeping generalisation. There are a few exceptions, he says, like the Marquee, Middle Earth, Manor House and Birmingham Mothers, but they are in the minority.

There are other reasons, too, for the big group exodus to the States.

"The basic reason is the lack of exposure," says Jimmy. "There just aren't the big

Left

Page works his violin

bow technique, whilst

Right

demonstrating his 'wah-

wah' effects pedal

Opposite

Bonham, Plant and Page

relax with 'Oz' (the

underground mag of the

sixties)

venues in which to play. What is needed is a club in every major city which is something between the size of the Marquee and the Roundhouse.

"Like the Cream and Hendrix got to the stage where they needed gigantic places. They could get a 6,000 audience with ease and there was nowhere to accommodate them.

"Any group that plays the Albert Hall is out of its head because of the acoustics."

These are the crucial reasons why Led Zeppelin – surely the most exciting new talent to emerge from these shores for many months – will be spending six months of every year in America, with the rest for holidays and work in Britain and Europe.

It is a sad commentary on the state of British pop.

But one way or another – even if it is from across the Atlantic – we will be hearing a lot more of Led Zeppelin.

Outstanding

The group's first LP was released by Atlantic last Friday and is an outstanding achievement, even without consideration of the fact that it was cut in just 30 hours, only three weeks after their formation.

Most of the ideas are Jimmy's, but behind his singing guitar the drums of John Bonham and the bass and organ of John Paul Jones are remarkably together, while Robert Plant's stimulating vocals give the depth of an extra instrument.

The success of the album in the States, coupled with their debut tour, has led to Led Zeppelin being talked of as a second Cream in terms of earning power and musicianship.

"There is a comparison in that Zeppelin, like Cream, was picked from the best musicians available at the time," says Jimmy. "But I don't play anything like Eric. I am nowhere near as good. I am still learning."

Having taught himself guitar since he was 13, Jimmy began doing session work at the age of 19. He was the youngest session man around until John Paul Jones, fellow Zeppelin, came on the scene and beat him by a year.

The experience Jimmy gained from having to force himself to adapt to different styles - a bit of jazz, a bit of classical - plus his work with people like Mick Jagger, Eric Clapton, Kinks and Donovan proved a valuable apprenticeship towards his status as one of Britain's leading guitarists.

A friend of Jeff Beck since he was 11, Jimmy joined the Yardbirds in 1966 after becoming disillusioned with session work and realising its restrictions. "When it came to playing solos I never had any."

Eventually replacing Beck when he left, Jimmy stayed with the group for two years until last summer when the Yardbirds split. Jimmy, the "new boy," was the only one left.

It is interesting to note that Jimmy's individual guitar style derives in part from the care he takes not to fall into the trap of sounding like Clapton or Hendrix.

"There are lots of little standard phrases that everyone recognises as Clapton's or Hendrix's. It is trying to get original phrases that makes it interesting."

I left Jimmy to collect his luggage for the trip to Bolton where Zeppelin were appearing that night. I hope the good people of the north listened that evening - because if they listened they couldn't help but like.

And Led Zeppelin is a group we can't afford to lose.

How they got Led Zeppelin off the ground...

Royston Eldridge July 5, 1969

Out in the windy wilds of Willesden, a not-so-salubrious part of North London, Britain's heaviest band are cutting tracks for their second album before they return to the United States.

Jimmy Page, John Paul Jones, Robert Plant and John Bonham have been together for less than a year as Led Zeppelin, yet they rate supergroup status in America and are talked of on this side of the Atlantic as "the new Cream."

Tapes

At the end of a lengthy session at the studios, ex-Yardbird Jimmy collected the tapes that represented another day's work and set off home.

On the way to his Thames-side house at Pangbourne, he talked of the past, present and future of Led Zeppelin.

It was getting on for midnight but Jimmy was wide awake. The session that they had just completed was nothing compared with the normal Zeppelin marathons which usually start mid-evening and go on until the early hours of the following day.

Rock

"We've cut tracks for this album both here and in the States. It's just a matter of time, fitting in what we can where we can. There's a lot of rock tracks on it; it's just a matter of juggling with what we've got.

"We're going back to the States and we'll be there until August 3. This will be our third trip since the group started. Since we've only been here for three months at the most, that's probably why we've got a bigger name over there.

"Everywhere we played before we went over last time was really great though. We played places like the Marquee and Klooks Kleek where there were more people turned away than there were inside."

Name

"The response at the concerts has been fantastic, too. The last concerts with Mick Abrahams and Liverpool Scene were really good. I think it's taken a long time to get a name over here because, like Ten Years After, we just haven't been here for most of the time.

"I'm really knocked out with this album - we've got quite a lot of stuff. Everything, except for one track 'Killing Floor,' is our own and we've done a really different arrangement on that.

"My influence? I've listened to everybody and every style of music. I appreciate all types of music, I like Bert Jansch, Joni Mitchell..Richie Havens, I like him, there's a lot of people...

Progressive

"Yes, the Yardbirds were very influential. The split came at the end of last summer when there was Jim, Keith and Chris Dreja and myself left. They were one of the first R & B groups and really got into the progressive thing at the end."

In view of Led Zeppelin's tremendous Stateside success has Jimmy considered making America the group's home?

"No, I wouldn't like to be based

in the States. American audiences let you know whether they like something straight away - halfway through a drum solo or something there's uproar, whereas here they really let you know at the end of the act.

"I was talking to Three Dog Night and they were very disturbed about the reaction they were getting here. I told them not to worry. They couldn't get used to the audience reaction at the end.

"Everywhere that you play it's like a new challenge. I'd like to work all over, Australia and Japan and so on. You have to work just as hard wherever you go. You know, England has really produced some fantastic things in all spheres of rock from blues groups to string bands. It really floors the Americans.

"They keep on saying 'where do all those amazing guitarists keep coming from?' They haven't really got that many at the moment - Jimi Hendrix, I suppose, but even the Americans think of him as being British."

Jimmy joined the Yardbirds because he felt that session work can be stultifying. The Yardbirds split eventually because they wanted to go in different directions. Was Jimmy now happy with

Led Zeppelin's development?

"It's going really well. We've got much closer together musically during the past few months. The policy of the band is that if someone wants to go off at a tangent everyone else would follow.

"Now we can feel these things easier, it's much more relaxed. I'm really enjoying playing.

Top

Page 'White Summer'

solo on Dan Electro

guitar, Royal Albert Hall,

1969

Left

Vintage Jimmy Page

USA 1969

Singular Success

The year opened with the band unexpectedly in the US top 5 with a single - an edited version of 'Whole Lotta Love' from the second album. Released at the insistence of Atlantic Records, and against Zeppelin's own wishes, it nonetheless became a million seller. The UK record company all but got it on to the streets too, before manager Peter Grant stepped in and invoked a contract clause which gave him an absolute veto over British single releases. Grant said that the band were not happy with the edit-shortened track, and would record another song specifically designed as a UK single. In the event, this did not happen, and Zeppelin were to stick rigidly to the "no UK singles" rule for the rest of their career.

Stage-wise, they played two wildly successful US tours during 1970, plus a European jaunt (including a Danish date as 'The Nobs' to appease Eva von Zeppelin, who objected to the band's use of the family name!). Their major UK appearance was at the open-air Bath Festival in June - a watershed gig which fully clinched both home public acceptance and critical approval.

Zeppelin put the excitement back into pop

Nick Logan January, 1970

It isn't hard to understand the substantial appeal of Led Zeppelin. Their current two-hour plus act is a blitzkrieg of musically perfected hard rock that combines heavy dramatics with lashings of sex into a formula that can't fail to move the senses and limbs.

At the pace they've been setting on their current seven-town British tour there are few groups who could live with them on stage.

Friday night, the third stop of the tour, brought them back to London's Albert Hall for a two and a quarter hour solo marathon that completely destroyed the ever-weakening argument about British reserve.

Exercising control over the sell-out crowd from 8.15 when they took the stage until 10.30 when they left it, they provoked a response that could have been a flashback to an early Stones happening, with perhaps only the exaggerations of nostalgia supporting the latter in a comparison.

At the end of two 15-minute long encores, when the audience had been on its feet dancing, clapping and shouting for 35 minutes, they were still calling them back for more.

Electricity

It was an electricity that had been building up throughout the evening.

The Albert Hall suits the Zeps' style and they were in good form, working through a selection of their heavier numbers, of which "Dazed and Confused" is still a tour de force.

The slight frame of Jimmy Page, clad like a Woolworth's sales counter in Alf Garnett shirt, jeans and white plimsols, belies the fearsome aggression of his guitar, while the other side of his nature comes through on the intricate "White Summer" solo.

Midway through the set John Paul Jones switched to Hammond organ for a segment of quieter Led Zeppelin not previously heard on stage, before John Bonham's "Moby Dick" drum solo brought him a standing ovation.

But the Zeppelin's forte, the closing 20 minutes, were still to come and when it did, such was the rapport that when on "How Many More Times" Robert Plant sang "I want you all to put your hands together..." the audience en masse had done so before he'd finished the request.

Strutting about the stage with arrogance, Plant

is a most accomplished performer, drawing from the finest blues/soul-shouter traditions with a confidence out of line with his inexperience previous to Led Zeppelin.

His control is masterful; so much so that when he dragged out the lyric "I've got you in the s-s-s-sights of my gun," hesitating dramatically over the "s", the crowd was shouting back and filling in the missing word.

I spoke to "Sir" Jimmy Page after the show and he confessed that the whole band had suffered extreme nerves beforehand, mainly because people like John Lennon, Eric Clapton and Jeff Beck had requested tickets.

"But it was just like it was at the Albert Hall in the summer," said Jimmy, "with everyone dancing around the stage. It is a great feeling.

"What could be better than having everyone clapping and shouting along? It's indescribable; but it just makes you feel that everything is worthwhile.

"We'd actually finished 'How Many More Times' and were going into 'The Lemon Song' but the audience was still clapping so we just went into another riff and carried on for a further ten minutes."

The group's intention in doing solo shows of such length, says Jimmy, is so that if the audience wants it they can continue playing without having to worry about whether earlier support groups have overrun and how much time there is left. They've had hassles with hall managements on this point in the past, and Jimmy points out:

"Our sets have got longer and longer anyway. They are now always at least two

hours long - and that's without any extra numbers for encores. I really believe in doing as much as it is physically possible to...if the audience wants it.

"Sure it gets physically tiring, sometimes shattering, specially for Robert. I don't know how his voice stands up to it, particularly on long tours in the States with the flying and that.

'Cast-iron'

"The change of temperatures, altitudes and conditions does affect his voice significantly - it's like waking up croaky in the morning - but thankfully on the night he always seems to have the necessary power there. He must have a really cast iron vocal case."

Jimmy's idea when forming Led Zeppelin was to gather together musicians who could play hard rock but were able to "employ other facets" as well.

"I thought the first album was a good example of that. It had blues, acoustic numbers, progressive things and straight hard rock.

"But the full potential of the band has yet to be fully realised, specially John Paul Jones. He did come through on the second album, whereas the first was mainly me. People would recognise him and say 'That's a good bass part and

that organ is nice.'

"We intend to use more organ. You see everyone can play so many instruments. John Paul Jones can play all the keyboard things and I can play lots of string instruments and near enough everything except piano."

There may be a subtle change coming in their music says Jimmy, but he is at pains to point out that they won't let the band lose its guts and drive.

Surprisingly, he confessed that he had had no faith in the Led Zeppelin II album, which is currently at No 3 in the NME LP Chart, "probably because I'd lived with it for so long. I thought we'd boobed. But that's a purely personal view and there are some things I like on it.

"What gives me confidence is that as people have taken to the second album and I know the

Far Left

Onstage at The Royal Albert Hall, January 1970. This concert was professionally filmed for the band's use in a proposed television documentary. This never materialised

Below Left and Left

Jones and Plant 'windswept' at Zeppelin's milestone outdoor conquest at the Bath Festival, June 1970

Below

John Bonham captured backstage at the Bath Festival

material for the third is better, it follows in theory that it should be a much better album."

Happier than ever

say's Zep's John "Bonzo" Bonham annoyed by rumours of a break-up... Roy Carr July 4, 1970

John Bonham is an incredibly happy person. But if there is one thing that's apt to annoy Led Zeppelin's powerhouse drummer and arch-raver, it's the rumours currently doing the rounds of the group's impending break-up.

"I want to say here and now, that it's all utter rubbish," he was quick to emphasise when we met the other day.

"We're all happier now that we have ever been. And I want everyone to know it.

"At the moment, the four of us are enjoying making our third album, and taking it easy at home in between sessions.

"Just because we are doing it all very quietly, some idiot thinks that we have packed in, and so all those false rumours start to circulate."

"Bonzo," as he is affectionately known in the trade, was very quick to point out, "This can really turn out very nasty. For the kids read it in the music papers, and naturally they believe it. That's bad."

What was originally meant to be just a quiet informal chat, turned into close on five hours of continuous raving around the drinking haunts of London's West End.

As it was a hot sticky afternoon, and unfortunately past closing time in the pubs, it was decided that we should find comfort in some private

Next Page

Guitar and vocal interplay for Page and Plant, Bath 1970

hostelry. So it was all down to the Cottage, which as it turned out had already been invaded by others with the same thought.

Ice cold

Suitably equipped with flagons of ice-cold lager, John and I decided to roam down Litchfield Street, for an uninterrupted chat. As Mike the Camera followed us, John spoke eagerly about the forthcoming Led Zeppelin III album.

"On this album people are going to listen to each one of us. We are all writing so much better than before, and there will be much more inventiveness from the group as a whole.

"This time we are also doing some acoustic tracks apart from the familiar heavier stuff. You know," he continued, "we're all much closer than before.

"At the moment, we've got ten good tracks laid down, and we have yet to do a couple more. If they turn out O.K. then we'll stick 'em on the album. The way things are going it looks as though it's going to be a long one.

"But, again it's only going to be a single album. We are not going to do the expected double-album thing, simply because most of these are just padded out with studio left-overs. On the Zeppelin's albums, we only include what we all consider to be our very best material."

Unfortunately, Bonzo couldn't give me any song titles, because there aren't any. It seems they don't get around to giving their songs their official titles until they are written, recorded and ready for release. Apparently this is the last formality.

At this precise moment Mike the Camera came up to us and asked John to stop speaking for a few minutes. Apparently this altered the structure of the facial muscles and didn't make for good photographs. With a look of amazement, he obeyed.

After playing at Pop Stars, I then asked him about Lord Sutch and his Heavy Friends album which had been called by many "An unofficial Led Zeppelin album."

"You must be joking. Sutch is a great bloke, but he used our friendship to sell his album. I'll give you the full story.

"It started in the middle of last year in Los Angeles," he began.

"We were in this club enjoying ourselves and so was Dave Sutch. Well, he came over to the table and we started talking about old times.

"During the course of the conversation, Sutch mentions how he's been in the business for years but never had the chance to actually cut an album, and that he really wanted to try and get one out in the States.

"He then asked Jimmy and myself if we would do a few backing tracks for him. But on the complete understanding that under no circumstances would he mention our names. As we had a couple of days to spare, we agreed.

"But it now seems as though he really took us in. He knew the position we were in, so we did it purely as backing musicians and old friends, NOT as Zeppelin. And this is what we did, we played as session-men and not as we would in our own group.

"When we arrived at the studio he said he

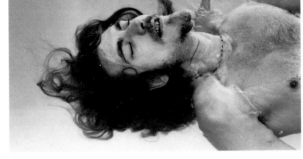

mainly wanted to do souped-up versions of old rock standards. So we said O.K. that sounds fine. What we didn't know was that when Sutch came to dub on the vocals in our absence, he had rewritten entirely different lyrics so that 'Lucille' became 'Thumpin' Beat' and Roy Head's 'Treat Her Right,' reappeared as 'Baby Come Back.' You've only got to play the album to spot where the other songs originated from.

"We didn't even notice that photographs were being taken during the sessions. Everyone did that album as a special favour to Sutch, and didn't want any credit. But as it turns out he deliberately used all the people's names to sell the album.

"So you can believe how amazed we all were when we saw our names in bold type all over the cover."

With all the false rumours circulating you can certainly discredit any that reach your ears about Zeppelin planning to replace Robert Plant with the electioneering Lordship.

John is very proud of Led Zeppelin and its achievements and rightly so. As a matter of interest he told me exactly how they came into being.

"Jimmy Page originally asked me to join the Yardbirds. In fact, Jimmy, Robert, John and myself actually played in Scandinavia as the New Yardbirds.

"The group proved to be so good that there and then we all decided to start afresh with a new name. On our return to London Keith Moon came up with the name Led Zeppelin, but nobody would give us a decent booking.

"We were getting offers of £25 a night. So we went to the States for our first tour

and that was it."

Suddenly a cloudburst cooled the heat of the day, so we retired to the Cottage. Once back inside, Bonzo started feeding a handful of tanners into a brightly lit "Bally De Luxe Gold cup" machine.

To yells of delight, Three-Of-A-Kind appeared in the score frames and the grand sum of twelve bob was John's. But alas, lady-luck did not smile on him after all because the machine refused to pay up.

After much arguing with the barmaid and a rather odd lager-swilling woman who kept on shouting and poking her nose in, we left minus John's winnings.

A Volkswagen Beetle isn't designed to accommodate six, but we managed it. With the windows rolled down we sped through Soho shouting words of admiration to all the many gorgeous young girls in their flimsy summer dresses.

Arriving at the Coach & Horses we were re-joined by publicist Bill Harry in company with the debonair Stan Webb of Chicken Shack fame and his manager, Harry Simmonds.

Suddenly Bonzo spied a poster advertising the appearance of Eric Clapton. So with glasses held high we all posed in front of it as the moment was captured for posterity on film.

Zeppelin film

On the subject of film, John spoke about the forth-coming Led Zeppelin movie.

Left

Classic Bonham close-up, onstage Bath 1970

Above

Page sports 'Farmer Giles' image whilst displaying 'bowing' techniques, Bath 1970

Previous page

Plant relaxes 'poolside' (top right) and performing onstage (below), USA 1970

"It will probably be an hour-long semi-documentary and will include some footage from the Royal Albert Hall concert.

"One of the highlights of the film will be a sequence featuring my 4-year-old son Jason playing his drums.

"He's got a completely scaled down replica of my kit, and believe me he can already play them."

John is very proud of his offspring, and his biggest long-term ambition is to have Jason play on stage with Led Zeppelin at the Royal Albert Hall. But before that there is their much-awaited appearance at the Bath Festival.

"To put a complete end to all the break-up rumours. Anyone who goes to the Bath gig will see and hear Led Zeppelin play as they've never heard us play before.

"We are all really looking forward to that date. In fact we are getting very excited about it. It's going to be a fantastic day, I can assure you."

150,000 Fans Pack Shepton Mallet

from NME Bath Festival review by

Roy Carr July 4, 1970

Until you have actually seen 200,000 (sic) people leap to their feet and start writhing and dancing, you can't imagine what a spectacle it can be. Well this is what happened during Led Zeppelin's show-stopping act.

John Bonham had previously told me that "Anyone who goes to Bath will see and hear Zeppelin play as they've never heard us play before", and he wasn't underestimating.

As expected, Led Zeppelin were the hit of the whole event, but not for their name value or past track record...it was because they played like no other band can. They have no equal.

Anticipation had built up all day, but prior to their actual appearance, it was all down to their manager Peter Grant who brought order and sanity to the chaotic stage area.

While Robert Plant strutted around the stage singing his throat-tearing vocals, Jimmy Page in a long overcoat and bush hat gave a free lesson to any guitarist fortunate enough to be watching.

John Paul Jones doubled expertly on bass and Hammond organ, while Bonzo thrashed his drums

with controlled abandon, his bass drum patterns are just incredible.

Following Bonzo's solo on "Moby Dick" and "How Many More Times", they encored with "Whole Lotta Love", everyone going berserk as they threw dozens of tambourines into the crowd and invited them to join in.

Insatiable

The throng was now insatiable and devoured a rock medley of "Long Tall Sally" which featured Bonzo standing on his drum stool clapping his hands above his head.

As they swung into "Say Mama" and "Johnny B.Goode" rockets were again ignited and the roar of the crowd was deafening.

Nothing could follow that.

Far Centre, and Below

Page and Plant pose in hotel

rooms pre-gig

Above

View from behind stage, USA 1970

Stairway to the World

Zeppelin identification on its enigmatic sleeve. It quickly, however, became their biggest seller yet, not least due to the inclusion of the anthemic 'Stairway To Heaven', the most consistently popular track the band would ever record.

Ireland unites under Zeppelin

The world's top rock band hits the road – and MM's Chris Welch goes with them to file this exclusive report

March 13, 1971

As their third album, Led Zeppelin III, descended from the number one slot on both sides of the Atlantic at the begining of 1971 – despite having fallen victim to harsh reviews and general press backlash at the band's apparently easy rise – Zeppelin were already busy recording its successor. Release of the fourth set was eventually heldback until November, however, by which time European, American, Japanese and two UK tours had confirmed Zeppelin as the hottest and hardest-working stage attraction in rock. The new album was cleverly marketed, with a minimalist visual approach. It had no title, apart from four runic symbols (one chosen by each member), and carried no group photo or any kind of

A new kind of riot hit Ireland last weekend. A riot of fun, laughter and excitement, when Led Zeppelin paid their first visit to the troubled isle.

The Britons who brought guitars instead of guns were given an ecstatic welcome. Cheering fans in Belfast and Dublin knew no barriers when it came to appreciating the return of the world's greatest rock band.

Zeppelin have been off duty for several

Far Left

'Back To The Clubs Tour' UK 1971

Right

Page – A study in concentration

Below

Out-take from a publicity shot

months. But they tour into their new round of appearances with electrifying exuberance.

Violence and explosions raged only half a mile away from their concert in Belfast on Friday night. But the young people of the town, unconcerned with ancient conflicts, used their energy to celebrate the worthwhile cause of peace, love and music.

In Dublin cheering fans jammed the National Boxing Stadium and gave the group an equally fervent welcome on their first trip to the divided country.

Zeppelin enjoyed themselves hugely, and responded with concerts which not only displayed their undoubted power and ability to incite an explosive response, but their musical taste and creativity.

Rare chemistry

Zeppelin unashamedly go out to entertain. They also happen to play fine songs injected with feeling, producing a rare chemistry.

As Robert Plant says: "We're all different personalities, but there is a kind of magic when we

get together again."

And Robert was just expressing his own pleasure at being back on the road with Jimmy Page, John Paul Jones and John "Bonzo" Bonham.

There are so many myths and misconceptions about Zeppelin. Because of their huge popularity and success, there are many who view them with a cynicism and snobbery.

But from the evidence assailing my at ears their "live" concerts, the band are more involved in music, more determined to progress than many an album chart rival.

Their current tour takes them to many of the small clubs where they started their success story - like London's Marquee.

But the first two dates took them to pastures new, and the reaction made them wish they had gone to Ireland from the earliest.

The fans in Belfast were particularly knocked out and grateful that Zeppelin flew in, as so many English bands have chickened out of the trouble-torn town.

In fact there was trouble - a petrol tanker was hijacked, a youth was shot dead and the inevitable fire bombs were hurled on the night we were in town.

By some miracle none of this was in evidence. All I saw on arrival at Belfast airport was a British soldier in a jeep who looked like Lethbridge-Stewart of Dr. Who.

And students from Queen's University were holding hilarious rag day festivities, flour-bombing passers-by and parading in warpaint.

The first concert was held in the Ulster Hall where a certain clergyman often spouts rabble-rousing rubbish.

But on Friday night all was purity and truth. The purity of youthful enthusiasm and the truth of rock and roll.

An electric atmosphere generated in the hall as Belfast boys and girls literally ran to their seats.

The determined, battering riff of "Immigrant Song," shook stage and floor as the band steamed in. Robert Plant, impressive in black and red

blouse, and golden hair with a demonic smile echoed through the towering speaker columns.

John Paul throbbed, Bonzo broiled and Jimmy jammed - it was good to hear them again.

All had complained about being "rusty," from the long lay-off. It didn't show. They attained a clean sound, free of distortion, with plenty of PA

echo that Robert uses with cunning effect. And they all seemed sparked by the crowd's ecstatic enthusiasm to bring new life to old favourites - "Heartbreaker," "Since I've Been Loving You," "Dazed and Confused," and their anthem "Whole Lotta Love."

Storms of applause greeted "Since I've Been Loving," the slow, measured marathon with its grandiose chord sequence. Here Jimmy played some beautifully fluent blues choruses, and ignited responding power from Bonham, executing potent fill-ins on drums and Apollo project accuracy and power.

There was plenty of new material - songs from the fourth album, which threatens to be possibly their best yet.

"Black Dog,"is a heavy rocker in the grand tradition, with typical Zep bass guitar and bass drum teamwork behind Page's aggressive guitar.

Much cheering greeted the new song and they quickly followed up with "Dazed," complete with menacing intro, Bonzo's gong reverberating behind John Paul's walking bass and Jimmy's wah-wah.

The violin bow episode extracted every ounce of high drama, and Jimmy even managed to obtain a passable imitation of the violin sound.

Another new song, "Stairway to Heaven," featured Jimmy on double-necked guitar, which gives him a 12-string and 6-string sound on the same instrument. An excellent ballad, it displayed Robert's developing lyricism.

Then came "Moby Dick," featuring the one and only John Bonham - the Compleat Drummer. Said Robert: "Here comes something that gets just that little bit better every night."

Marathon

John edged forward on his stool, crouched down and tore into his marathon. His hi-hat jigged a

merry dance, while his colossal bass drum rumbled to a climax. He played with his bare hands and his sticks. Bursts of applause punctuated the phenomenal feats of sweat and dexterity.

The ovation which greeted this performance prompted Robert to say: "A lot of those musical papers that come from across the sea say we are going to break up. Well - WE'RE NEVER GOING TO BREAK UP!"

A roar went up and the band triumphantly launched into "Whole Lotta Love."

From then on the audience began to approach hysteria as the band piled on the excitement, with "Boogie Mama," and "Communication Breakdown." Fans rushed the stage as the lights went up. "If we could all be like this every minute of every day there would be no more hang-ups, no problems," said Robert, and everybody knew what he meant.

For ten minutes the audience chanted for more, and just as a worried looking usher was saying: "Please boys and girls - the concert is over," Zeppelin returned.

"They really were fantastic," said a local girl, Anita, outside their dressing room later. "And are they an English band? I always thought they were from America. I always thought Robert Plant was fat and Jimmy Page was tall from a picture I have at home. You get these funny notions."

After the concert the group and manager Peter Grant drove in various cars across the Border to Dublin, where we were due to check-in at the Inter-Continental Hotel.

John Bonham had his own car and actually

Below

Jones (top) and Bonham (below).

The rhythm section in harmony

November 1971. Their unique under

current provided a basis for much

improvisation

Far Right

Zeppelin turn up the heat on a cold

November night, Wembley 1971

drove by mistake right through the notorious Falls Road riot area.

Berserk

"The street was covered in glass and there were armoured cars and kids chucking things," he said later. "We just kept our heads down and drove right through."

The Dublin concert was held in the boxing stadium and a new stage had to be constructed specially during the afternoon to accommodate all Zeppelin's equipment.

It was another triumph, although Dublin was just a little slower than Belfast in getting into the spirit of the occasion.

By the end of the evening, with Robert roaring into an improvised rock medley, Dublin went just as berserk as their friends north of the border.

As a bonus for the crowd they played "Summertime Blues," with Atlantic records executive Phil Carson jamming on bass guitar.

"I enjoyed Ireland, and wish we could come back," said Jimmy, feeling tired and just a little ill, on the plane back to London.

"We're not playing the great long three-hour shows now, but like to give a good balanced programme, with new and old material.

As our Trident bumped over the choppy Irish Sea, Jimmy talked about the new songs and Led Zeppelin Four.

"On the LP John Paul Jones has over-tracked recorders on the introduction to 'Stairway to Heaven,' which we can't reproduce on stage, but the acoustic guitars come off well. The words are brilliant - they are probably the best Robert has ever written.

"The album is almost finished. We recorded some of it on location with a mobile truck and got a really good atmosphere. Actually the words of one song relate to earthquakes, and right after we did the number, the earthquake happened in California - which was a bit unnerving!

"I don't know if that song will go on the LP - ('Going to California'), nobody wants to drop

anything. All the songs we have done hold up.

"We used the Rolling Stones' mobile recording truck which we parked outside a house, while we played inside. We had the drums in the hall and we sat around the fire and played our guitars.

"Bonzo got a big and fat drum sound. I expect you notice the sound of the drums often gets strangled in a studio.

"We have all contributed to the writing, but there is no point in trying to explain all the numbers. You'll have to listen to the LP. It would be really

nice to do a double album and maybe get the truck out to record some 'live' gigs.

"It's really good to be back playing gigs again. It was a kind of instant excitement on the first concert. I was wondering what it would be like. There is a danger that if the fans get too excited that you can't get the acoustic numbers across. That's all we ever want - a chance to get all of our music across. We've got four albums of material now to choose from, and I think we get a pretty good balance.

Kick

"I still get a great kick out of playing 'Dazed And Confused' and the 'Immigrant Song.'"

When will the new album be out and what is it to be called?

"We don't know yet - sometime in April. It might be called Zeppelin Four. Everybody expects that, but we might change it. We've got all sorts of mad ideas. I was thinking at one time of having four EPs. But we want to keep the price down and frankly the price of records now is extortionate. The only way we can make it up is to give more playing time.

"And with this sort of music, the whole thing is to get as much 'level' as you can, so the record sounds as good on any kind of player. If the level is down, you may lose a lot of bass sound. You have to check all that in the cutting stages and in quality control."

Is there any particular mood to the album?

"Well, 'Stairway' is a pretty good representation of what we are doing now. There are different moods to the song which lasts ten or twelve minutes. We want to do a really long track one day, but not yet. There is quite a lot of instrumental as well."

I mentioned to Jimmy that Led Zeppelin were comparatively quiet on their gigs compared to many a noisier band.

"We have been trying to cut down on volume. There are so many complaints about volume, and people have been linking us with Grand Funk Railroad, and I can't see any comparison at all. It really hurts to be compared to a band which is just volume. We did

Left, Right

Stark stage settings enhance Plant's

dramatic action onstage at Empire

Pool, Wembley, November 1971.

Plant's classic rock star poses would

be much imitated in years to come

acoustic things on our first album, and I would have thought that would have created a precedent for us. I've never heard Grand Funk Railroad get into that kind of thing.

"We know where we are going as a group. We are four individuals who have found a common denominator in music. There was a lot of inspiration coming through on this new album. We're getter better all the time."

Zapped by Zeppelin
Roy Hollingworth at Wembley Pool
November 27, 1971

I'll bet nearly every critic who witnessed Led Zeppelin at the Wembley Pool last Saturday night will have a bag full of put-downs next to his typewriter this week.

I'll also bet that among London's rock society there will be talk of "disappointment." When you're Britain's biggest band, you get the heaviest critics. If Jesus was still about, we'd expect a miracle every week. Right?

But no matter what the rock society says. What matters are people. An entertainer performs for people. He is not an entertainer if he performs to critics. Led Zeppelin performed to the people on Friday night, and 9,000 of them put their hands above their heads, and got their Saturday night rocks off.

This was an English band playing like crazy, and enjoying every minute they stood there on stage. They played non-stop for the best part of three hours. Enormous. They played about everything they've ever written. Nothing, just nothing was spared. This was no job, this was no "gig". It was an event for all. So they get paid a lot of bread. Well, people paid that bread, and I'll reckon they got every penny's worth. It was a great night actually. Great. Christ - there was the breakthrough of Stone the Crows as well.

Early evening: Wembley Central tube station is dark and shiny wet. An incredibly cold evening, an angry wind, and rain as sharp as acid. The tubes are full of polite long-hairs and ladies, as are the platforms, as is the road to Wembley stadium. If you run you dodge spots. So everyone runs a little. There's the rip-off merchants with the duff programmes. They don't appear to be making it. Then there's the stadium, warm and busy. The stalls that follow rock and roll. The rock and roll market, right there in Wembley, and looking as established as if they'd been there for years. The T-shirts, the incense, the posters. The casual, polite movements. Oh, and Jeff Dexter serving music from his little tower to the left of the stage. We've built our own little world, you know. It just so happens to be music that fronts it.

your ears. It helps."

Then Farr. "We've been asked if there's an official programme. Well there isn't. But we've got beautiful souvenir posters instead. They're printed on heavy paper, so you can keep them a time." He's not asking 50p for them, not 40p - but 30p. "You can have a beautiful poster. Ladies and gentlemen, Stone the Crows."

What an unbelievable set they played. This was the best set they've ever played. And what a fine night to pick. At last we've fully seen what Stone the Crows are all about,

and what they're about is just great. There was Les Harvey playing guitar like he's never played it before. He went mad, and Maggie Bell was just proud that Saturday evening, prouder than she's ever been. It all worked. There's been a thin shell holding something back, and that shell shattered, and out flew the Crows. Soul and blues, and soul, and grit and some thoroughly

It's an exciting occasion. Here we are at home with Led Zeppelin, comfy on a cold, perishing English night. The well-known character Rikki Farr takes the stage, weaving his way through an army of roadies. You can see he's going to say something, but it's Dexter who speaks first. "You people at the front. We're sorry it's so loud. All I can say is go and get some bog paper, stuff it in

mean conditions that cut through the air loud and thick, and ridiculously tight.

It was on from the start. It's one of these nice things about bands, you can see them visually making it. You can see some change coming over them. You can see something that's been nurtured, been held down, suddenly come out. During the first length, Harvey was bouncing about so much his strap leapt off, and Maggie walked about in her gipsy dress, sizzling and conscious that something very pleasant was happening.

Mid-evening: Performing pigs. Circus acts, beasts that do clever things are brought out for the audience's amusement..It's like the Roman games. It's travelled a long way

Above

Page and onstage

equipment featuring

Runic symbols from

fourth album sleeve

Below

Jones plays Fender

Jazz Bass

Opposite

Plant's vocals soar sky

high at Wembley, 1971

from the compere who had a sleeve-full of bad jokes. Now it's the rock 'n' roll circus. What startling entertainment. Did you see a pig on a trampoline? It just needed a Christian or two thrown to the lions. Great.

There's a wonderful hum in the air as the minutes tick away towards Led Zep. You can see the band backstage, itching to play. You can tell, you can feel that. There's people in such great moods. Everyone, just everyone is raving about the Crows, they've warmed everything up so well. Everyone wants more. Zep manager Peter Grant walks about surrounded by a flock of his children. The audience are taking their seats.

The stewards, elderly, uniformed finish their canteen of mashed potatoes and beans in the hall backstage. "I've been working here for 'X' years, and I've never known such happy, polite people," says one. "Everyone says please, and everyone says thank you, I want to see this group, THE Zeppelin."

So now the lights are dipping, and from the blocks of people that rise above eye level there comes the mumble of someone on the verge of getting what he's been waiting for. A minute of very silent silence, several electrical "zaps" as leads are connected.

It's going to be very very loud..."Brammmm," and the air shivers, and you feel your eardrums being pushed inwards like sails full of wind, and there in the light is Jimmy Page, playing his guitar low-down, and fast and quick, and he rushes to the front of the stage, and

there's the most beautiful cheer. And then Robert Plant puts the stick to his mouth, and screams, yes he screams, and it's so loud it's dangerous. And Bonham blats, blat, blat, and that's like thunder. You can feel the force of the combined volume hit you physically. It's painful, but it rips out an emotion common to most everyone in the hall. Excitement, and something rude, something so alive it smells. Rebel-rousers, that's it. It's not pretty, it's not to be sat and listened to, it's to be absorbed and thrown back. It's to be used as a dose of something that brings out energy. You can know everything about rock, but can you still enjoy it?

"Good evening," shouts Plant. "Good evening" roars the audience. My, how fat John Bonham gets, as he tightens up screws.

Jimmy Page, I remember the first time I saw him, on one of his first gigs with the Yardbirds, in a mid-sixties marquee in the middle of some scrub land in Derby. He was in a white suit, and he stood back and scrubbed six strings till they blurred, and the sound was like one great marching wall. The lady who was on my shoulders fell off, and the marquee went mad. On Saturday Jimmy stood back, and did that same scrub, with John Paul Jones holding it steady with a one note bass run.

Then Page attacked again, it's showmanship. He curls it all down silent, then barks out like an electric dog with loads of sharp bits of bone in his mouth. He lapses into a classic run, and then a selection from "59th Street Bridge Song"(!). He moves well, all the tricks, sneaking about. It's a gorgeous action to watch. Meanwhile Plant is still screaming. Maybe it's too loud, but maybe it's not. It's obscene.

If you were devoted fully to being critical then you could see things that aren't perfect. If you're capable of feeling what an audience feels, if you're capable of watching, and without inhibitions, enjoying, then those faults slip away. There's something to watch all the time. During the times you're not satisfied musically, you can be satisfied emotionally. You can also be satisfied visually. You can also get the warm feeling of watching one of the world's biggest bands playing to its own audience. Just like it should be.

Plant has this remarkable voice. You could easily hate it. Hear it on an album, and I just might, but "live" it figures. It's good, living stuff. "Black Dog," and he wails, and the voice becomes an instrument. It's amplified to such an extent that it becomes no human hollering, but a confusion of electrical deformities that gropes outwards, and trespasses on nearly every inch of your thoughts. There's this clattering coming from Bonham. "Since I've Been Loving You," and Page takes a 12-string, and shimmers out a belling tone.

Acoustic

Plant feels it. So his voice ain't necessarily hip. But he feels it, oh he feels it. It's no sham. It's meant.

"Rock 'n' Roll," and Pagey walks about with his guitar like it were just another limb. He's sweaty now, they're all sweaty, and the audience is getting sweaty. So Zep sit down a while, and go acoustic: "Going to California," and it becomes soft.

It's Page and Plant drifting into calmer realms. A handful of calm songs, and then another handful. My, this is a long set. Plant sounds like Donovan with a headcold, but the acoustic break is colourful. Right.

Back to the electrics. Pagey takes a bow, and bows his guitar, beats it with the bow, and the reverb is unnatural. You can't believe he's actually making the sound that comes out. Then "Celebration Day," and another 12-string solo from Page. Time passes.

Now the mikes at the front of the stage stand alone, like signals with no trains. There's nobody front-stage, just this blamming from the rear. The Bonham solo bullets through minutes, and ten minutes, and more. A standing ovation, well it's more than that. Nobody could wish for a better ovation.

Time passes into "Whole Lotta Love," and the whole thing burns onwards. It's getting near the end, it's been a colossal set timewise, but there will have to be an encore, and without hesitation there is "Goodbye Mary Lou," and other playful things. Then the end. And, yes, the encore. Then 9,000 people get up and say thanks.

And went outside and got wet.

The Trek Continues

No new album was released this year, though Zeppelin began album recording sessions again in April and, during a short stay in India in February, Jimmy Page also made some experimental recordings with members of the Bombay Symphony Orchestra. For the rest of the year, the band were hardly off the road, touring widely in Australia and New Zealand, Japan, the US (their eighth such stint), Europe (just a pair of dates in Montreux, Switzerland), and the UK - where 120,000 tickets sold out as soon as the 18-city end-of-year trek was announced. The fifth album was actually completed in time for this latter tour, but failed to appear on schedule because its front sleeve picture (shot at the Giant's Causeway in Ireland, and not actually involving Zeppelin themselves) was running into continual delays as its photographic and colour processing details failed to meet the band's exacting criteria.

How Robert Plant stays fresh

"We don't flog Zep to death" - Roy Carr, April 29th 1972

Led's larynx, Robert Plant, exudes an enthusiasm for his vocation that one rarely encounters among the rock hierarchy.

Why, only the other afternoon I encountered the man himself and Zeppelin's Master-at-Arms, Richard Cole, conducting a rip-off raid on Kinney Records' vast library of tapes and albums and the singer conceded that: "Music is serious...but let's dig it."

"Arthur Alexander...now there's a name to conjure with," he smiled as the smooth voice of the almost-forgotten rhythm and blues singer filled the large room and obliter-

ated all nearby conversation.

Accepting a welcome drink, Plant carefully removed the filter from a cigarette and confessed:

"You know what? This record sounded much better then than it does now."

He was of course referring to a time in the early sixties when the style and songs of Mr. Alexander and his contemporaries helped, in some small measure, to blue-print the format of those British groups who were to completely change the entire course of rock music.

In fact I have the strangest feeling that at one time or another a rather younger Robert Plant possibly offered his own interpretations of "Anna" or the like around the noisy Brummie club and ballroom circuits.

"For me, in fact, the most successful concert is the one when everyone is up on the feet, smiling, yelling and getting into the music.

"Personally I don't like things to be too straight-faced. The idea of people just sitting down and getting turned on without showing any signs

Right

Jones captured during organ solo

Left

Page and Plant in action

Below

Rare rehearsal shot at Rainbow

Theatre, London 1972

of response - it's just too melodramatic.

"The fact is, we don't flog Zep to death. Just like John Lennon once said: 'If you're on the road too long it becomes painful'."

Plant further echoes the sentiments of the band's drummer, John Bonham, in pointing out that Zeppelin have set their own pace, one which allows them sufficient freedom and creativity.

He told me: "Speaking for myself I've always got the motivation to work, but like the rest of the band I don't want to charge around the country every night. What's the point?

"We only tour and bring out an album when we want to. But as most people realise, we're always popping up all over the world to do concerts. Whenever possible we always return to those places."

Plant is proud, and quite rightly so, of Led Zeppelin's past achievements.

"We were the first band to take over and play the Empire Pool, Wembley, and present non-rock side features like circus acts - although the pigs didn't quite manage to get it on," he referred with a laugh to one of the interludes at the memorable Wembley bash.

Of the four Led albums - all of which immediately turned gold - it was their fourth which for the first time minutely revealed the full spectrum of their collective talents.

"Music is very much like a kaleidoscope," said Plant. "And I feel that particular album was just a case of us stretching out. It was a very natural development for us.

"I like people to lay down the truth.

"No bullshit."

He told me: "In the case of 'Battle of Evermore' I had been reading a book on the Scottish Wars immediately before. It was really more of a playlette than a song, and after I wrote the lyrics I realised I needed another different voice, as well as my own, to

give that song its full impact. So I asked Sandy Denny along to sing on that track.

"I found it very satisfying to sing with someone who has an entirely different style to my own.

"While I sang about the events of the song, Sandy answered back as if she was the pulse of the people on the battlements.

"Sandy was the town-crier - urging the people to throw down their weapons.

"'Stairway to Heaven' was the result of an evening when Jimmy and I just sat down in front of the fire. We came up with a song which was later developed by the rest of the band in the studio."

Much of Zeppelin's appeal has been by virtue of their consummate ability to produce material hanging on instant riffs...a characteristic they developed to great lengths

on "Black Dog", which, to the annoyance of their plagiarists, includes instrumental passages which are almost impossible to copy.

"They're really atuned to all those time skips," Plant explained with devilish delight, "they" being the rest of the band. "These things aren't intentional, just little whims which we'll no doubt expand on the next album.

"When they're doing these kind of time skip riffs in the studio, Jimmy, John and Bonzo suddenly come up with something like that passage

on "Black Dog"; play it, fall about all over the place for about 10 minutes in fits of laughter, then preserve it on tape.

"It's as simple as that."

Sessions for the new album are under-way and, without disclosing any secrets, Plant did say that it would include some things of interest.

Like all major acts Led Zeppelin have suffered from bootlegs and in return attempts have been made to cut a live album officially (the last being during a recent tour of Japan) but Plant told me the sound balance was just as bad as the bootleg. It was therefore rejected as unsuitable.

He added wryly:

"You know, we've recorded ourselves at the Farm on just an ordinary Revox, and achieved a far better sound." There must be a moral in that statement.

And with that, he was up and off to grab another armful of albums.

Whole Lotta Led

Roy Hollingworth reports from New York   July 1st, 1972

The noise cajunked, and beefed outwards, filling each corner of the circular, space-aged Nassau Coliseum, Long Island, New York State.

Sixteen thousand people didn't know whether they were coming or going. Many danced, crazily, while others just stood, stared and smiled.

Led Zeppelin had been off stage four times. Four times they had fled under the archway to the side of the stage, and four times an unnatural din of screaming and cheering and unbelievable begging had brought them back out.

Now their set was approaching four hours in length – four incredible hours of the most wonderful music. Jimmy Page was on his toes, shaking and trying to pull out a last batch of magical notes. He'd pulled so many that evening, it seemed inconceivable that he could maintain such a peak. But something tricked him, and he spun round, ran across to Robert Plant, bursting, and slamming chords. Plant smiled, threw his head back, and the band rocked so hard you'd have thought there was no tomorrow.

Does anybody really know how big Led Zep are?

For four years Zep have been slaying America. For four years they have met with the dooming criticism that they could never do as well again, and yet they've come back, and done better. This present tour will more than likely go down as their best ever. They are playing better than they've ever played in their lives.

Strange how the Zep became unfashionable back home. Sure, they sell albums, and they can fill the Empire Pool - but where were all the trimmings, where was the real flash, the excitement? It was in the audience to be sure, but for some reason the media took it all with a pinch of salt. The fact that Led Zeppelin are possibly the biggest band in the world never figures. And that's a sad mistake.

It figures here, mind. Here Zep are truly recognised. Why do you think they come so often? Money, sure...But also because Zep are a band that love playing, and here there are no inhibitions. They find their audience. Here they play their best.

"The scenes have possibly amazed you," said John Paul Jones. "But this has been happening for four years now. I think we all feel a bit annoyed that nobody really knows it back home. Do they really know exactly what we're doing?"

This feeling is common within the band. Why, you might say, should they worry? They do well, the audience - which is the main thing - knows just how big they are. Why should they bother about wee small England and its fickle way?

Well they're English, and like most people, they also have egos. They'd just like England to know what they're doing.

"Our egos have been hurt," says Rob Plant.

"They really have. For some reason English critics have never told the truth about us. For some reason they've been out to get us a bit. So things are clouded over, and nobody gets to know what's really happening. There's been so much bullshit printed, it's just untrue."

"We read pages on some band - name not mentioned - saying just how big they are here. You ask the people here just how big they are. We know. You see it makes the English press look ridiculous. It's so annoying," added Jones. "Here we are slaving away, and getting consistently incredible reactions and nobody back home can care anything about us." He shook his head. "It's just not right."

"Maybe," said Plant, "if we were as big in England as we are here, I wouldn't be able to walk down a bloody street without being stopped," he laughed. "Don't know if I'd like that or not."

The scene was the Waldorf Astoria Hotel, on a sickening, heavy, hot New York day. Manager Peter Grant was stood with two house detectives in a corridor. His huge frame dwarfed them somewhat. There had been some trouble over the amount of people visiting "Bonzo Bonham's" room and, as per usual, a hotel had it in for the Limey longhairs.

The night before had seen the band play the first of two concerts at Nassau. They were overjoyed at how it had gone.

"Something has really happened this time," said Plant. "Something has really clicked. It's fantastic, the spirit within the band is just fantastic."

Plant is a cheery character, forever jigging, and rocking around, spreading a laugh or two with the first colourful Brummie accent I've ever heard. Talk centred on Wolves, and the rise to fame of Midlands football teams. Derby and Wolves could indeed rule, and it was a God almighty shame that Forest has sunk to such depths as relegation.

Page was quietly going about his business, and then in a fit of laughter Bonzo appeared. The grizzly King Drummer. An honest lad who likes to swing sticks like fury, and drink at about the same frantic pace.

"Y'um wouldn't believe what bloody trouble is goin' on with my room." It appears that trouble forever surrounds dear Bonzo.

Pretty soon the line of limousines was poking its way in and out of the absurd traffic towards Long Island. The three cars were in radio contact with each other, and the state of traffic soon decreed that somebody's house could not be visited. "Make sure the spare ribs are driven to the Coliseum," came a message over the radio.

Now the Coliseum is a strange building. It sits seemingly in the middle of nowhere, looming like a space research centre, circular and concrete.

Why didn't they play the Madison Square?

"Because it cost 5,300 dollars to book that place," says Peter Grant, "and that's just absurd. This is a great place, and this is where the kids live. Shame there aren't places like this in England. It's getting absurd over there now. There's nowhere to play.

"But we're going to be playing somewhere in England at Christmas," he said. "I think it will be good. I can't tell you where it is yet, but I think it will be good.

"You know I wanted to put the band on at Waterloo Station. You know, that massive area before the platforms. I thought it was a great idea - you know we could have Led Zeppelin specials coming in on the platforms, it was going to work, but the station authorities said there was one late train that would get in the way. Shame, it would have been great, imagine Led Zep playing Water-

loo Station - a completely covered hall, and very good acoustics.

The Coliseum was beginning to fill, and when I walked out with Plant he was met with a load of hand-shakers.

"Just want to say you're the best band in the world. You just are. I just want to say that," said one lad. "Ta very much," said Plant, and gave the guy a backstage pass. "You're the best band in the world," said another. And they really meant it.

Martin, one of the famous crew of Led Zepp roadies, was squeezing Plant's lemons in the dress-ing room. A half-dozen lemons, mixed with honey and tea to feed the Plant voice. How it kept going that night was amazing.

Bonzo was just carrying his sticks, and the clothes he's arrived in. "I got stopped backstage somewhere you know, and they wouldn't believe I was with the band. They said, 'where's your stage clothes', I said 'where's the what?...'"

The time was right, and the band made its way out of the room, and stood in a large hall backstage. The excitement just round the corner was thick as 16,000 people made ready. There was that hum, that frightening hum.

An electrical tone was started. It sounded like the rising drone of a bomber. It got louder, louder, till it filled the whole place, and the tone, the band walked onto the stage. The place collapsed, and the band, without hesitation kicked into rock. Page stabbed out a riff, and Plant yelled and squealed, and glory, all hell broke lose.

Page is the complete guitarist. He captures every emotion that sears through his head, and channels it through his arms. Whether it be a chord, a riff, or a gaggling neckful of notes, he is perfect.

And when technical ability might just swamp feeling, Page finds a dirty discord, and lets it cut ugly and messy through the tapestry. It sort of jerks your body and throws you, and then he finds a true line again, and weaves on in a straight, sharp direction. Their music has indeed got better. There appears to be a deal more open-ended excitement about the unit.

Page is in fine fettle, swaying on his heels, and then shaking his mass of hair into a blurr of tangles, which are picked up by the many spots and turned gold, and then white. Plant gets all very sexual, all mouths, heaves and sighs, and frenzied guttering

down the mike...And then he forces that screaming voice right out. Page ends the riff, Bonzo falls silent, Jones stops, and only Plant's crazy voice insults the silence.

Three acoustic numbers give people time to breathe, lie back and relax. John Paul Jones exhibited a new electric mandolin, that gave a good colourful feel to songs written on Welsh hillsides.

Then they all upped and left dear Bonzo.

He remained, and delivered the most wrecking drum solo you'd ever imagine. He beat the things so hard, with sticks and hands, that I thought his arms were going to fall off, or maybe the kit would shatter. His object was to reach grumbling thunder, and that he did, a sort of crazy stampede of drums, and sharp, slashed cymbals. It went on over 15 minutes and he wouldn't stop.

Bonzo would cool it all down to just one motion. Everyone knew exactly what Bonzo was playing, but he wasn't playing it - if you can see what I mean.

And then he struck back, and with no nerves at all just smacked everything till it hurt, and hurt. The tempo doubled, and doubled again, and his anguished face and black hair were wet through and streaked with burning skin and sweat.

"Someone once asked me what technicalities I applied to my playing," Bonzo had said to me. "I said, 'technicalities, what the hell are you going on about?' I said 'this is my technicality', and raised my hand into the air, and let it fall. Head to drum, that's what it is, head to drum.

"I'm not trying to be any superstar. I just do my bit as one quarter of Led Zeppelin. When I have a solo I don't ever imagine drummers around watching me. I don't try to impress people who play the drums. I play for people. I don't try and perform the most amazing changes in tempo, or make people watch me. I just couldn't do that - it would take away the essence of Jimmy's guitar, and Robert's voice. John Paul and myself lay down a thick back-drop, that's what we do."

The place was in a fever now of sheer adulation. It couldn't stop, and it didn't. The band stonked into "Whole Lotta Love," with Pagey

experimenting the bizarre with the reverb unit. He stood there, on his own, slashing and playing loud. Now we're backstage, and the band have run off, but Bonzo's saying they've got to do another, and the screaming is really painful on the ear from outside.

John Paul Jones takes the stage on his own, and sits at an organ. From that he delivers a medley of songs, some old, some new, some forgotten, and then into spine-chilling religious chords. It sounded like the Phantom organist, rushing forth with colossal organ chords, and then Jones broke into "Amazing Grace."

Soon all the band were back on stage, and Page laid a boogie out, and Plant growled "Boogie Mama," and what a boogie it was. It was like some stoked-up train belting on into the night - Bonzo being the pistons, Page the driver, it gouged into everybody's head.

Things were coming fast and furious. Next thing you know they're into "Peggy Sue," and a rock 'n' roll medley. And America goes wild, and dances.

So now we're back into the limousine again and Robert Plant is shaking his head. "They'd never believe how good it is here back home. They'd just never believe what happened tonight."

The way they had been applauded. The way the whole place had begged every last thing out of the band. The way the band had given everything they had, and still wanted to give more. Can you believe how big they are?

"They say Jethro Tull are brilliant on stage", said Jones, "well they do the same bloody thing every night, the same gags, everything the same. Each of our gigs is treated differently, we don't have any set, religiously rehearsed thing. And what you've seen tonight has been happening for years here."

It had been a most memorable evening. The memory of Plant there twisting and turning and screwing himself up on stage. Singing boogie, and singing rock, and singing ballad, and singing his heart ou. Of Page being THE guitarist, the rock guitarist, of Bonzo and HIS drums, and of John Paul Jones on the most pungent bass, and organ avec le difference.

And the audience loving every second of it like no audience I've ever seen.

Plant life

by Chris Charlesworth

November 11, 1972

In less than an hour Plant will be strutting across a stage every inch the rock and roll star, but in his Montreux hotel room overlooking Lake Geneva he's nothing more than a likeable guy from the Midlands, quick with his humour, sensitive to criticism and well experienced in the ways of the world.

Two years ago he was voted top male singer in the MM poll; this year he wasn't but he's a better singer now than he was then.

Why then, Robert, haven't Led Zeppelin played in this country recently ? "I believe we did something towards the beginning of this year at Wembley."

"But that was last year," I countered.

"Well, it was towards the beginning of this one. From there we had a little break, and went to Australia. We came back and had about three weeks off and then went to America, and we've

Previous Page,

Far Left

Plant shakes tambourine

during 'Stairway To Heaven',

Alexandra Palace, 1972

Previous Page,

Right, Top and

Bottom

Plant and Bonham display

colourful taste in velvet

stagetop

Left

'Bron-Yr-Aur Stomp',

Alexandra Palace, 1972.

This building was renowned

as the headquarters of BBC

Radio in London. The

acoustics did not suit live

rock concerts, but satisfied

12,000 fans who saw

Zeppelin over two nights

been recording over a period of time all the time.

"In between gigs we have always got studio time booked so the albums become a continuous thing. If we keep going in to recording studios a wider spectrum of stuff comes out of it."

Already there's enough material recorded for the next Zeppelin album, but problems with the sleeve have held things up. Now it looks as though January will see its release.

New album

"We can record as often as we want to, and Jimmy has a set-up at his place so the music is far more varied than it used to be.

"We will rehearse for a tour and get as many as four new numbers off in one day. It's just riffs coming out that we remember, like 'Black Dog' which was a riff.

"I'd like to think that each album is different from the last. If you imagine two lines on a tangent going outwards and getting wider, that's what we want our music to be. In about four years we will have covered all sorts of ground.

"There's a track on this new album called 'The Crunge' and it's really funny. It's something we would never have imagined doing. Numbers like this are really good because if you carry on on just one plane you just repeat yourself."

Plant isn't afraid that Zeppelin are in danger of being typecast into the heavy riff mould.

"No, people have identified us with the riffy numbers immediately because they are the most easily recognisable things. I think we should be known more for 'Stairway to Heaven' than 'Whole Lotta Love'."

Left

The Hammer of The Gods –

Bonzo enhances rhythm

section with timpani

percussion. From the early

days group members

would prevent him using

twin bass drums, such

was the force of his

playing style

Overleaf, left

'The Crowd Pleasers'

Below

Rock's golden Vocalist,

USA 1972

Did Plant agree that Zeppelin were becoming forgotten in England?

"There is definitely a pace that is apparent in England that is nothing to do with creativity. If you want to do it, you can keep up with everybody else and get your name in the papers as often as you can. That's done initially because artists like Elton John or T. Rex have something that is good and people have to be made aware of it.

"In England we could be around every week. It wouldn't be very hard to play once a month and it wouldn't be very hard to get our names in the papers if we went about it the right way by throwing our doors open to everybody in the press.

"'Do come up to the farm and see Robert Plant milking his goats' would get us in, but we've got a lot of places to visit and we like sightseeing. We don't want to have to keep up to that pace.

"People will soon remember us when they come and see us. We will be doing some gigs in England sooner or later, unless we happen to be playing in Basutoland or Zanzibar around Christmas.

"We've really got into going to places that most bands don't go to. We were among the first to go to Japan and the kids there show their appreciation in the most basic manner which is what it used to be like over here. Hong Kong is another place we want to play."

A musical change in Zeppelin is imminent when John Paul Jones starts using a Mellotron on stage, but the rock and roll medley at the close will stay in the act.

"We do it everywhere but it comes spontaneously. After the opening sequence I just start a song and hope everybody will catch on. I did 'Let's Jump The Broomstick' once, but we often put in 'Party', which is a really good one.

"When we did LA Forum we made some recording of the rehearsal, and we did about an hour's run-through which ended up getting an echo set going. I think we played every number on 'Elvis's Golden Discs Volume One'. It's amazing that you can stir yourself enough to get all the lyrics from that far back in time, and Jimmy managed to do all the right solos as well. It was all completely spontaneous.

"We were fiddling around once and we wrote a reggae number which will be on the next album, but I would like to have it out as a single."

The travelling around the world has brought music from all countries to the ears of Zeppelin, and Plant hopes to be able to make some recordings in Bangkok, a place he visited on the way home from Australia.

"Whether we could play there or not, I don't know because there are all sorts of political things happening like in Italy where there was tear-gas everywhere after the show. But you must move around and play to people who live in the outback as well as in America and England.

"I don't think we play England any less than America - it just seems that way at the moment.

"Some performers get very uptight about the press and a lot of groups get affected by this and won't play.

"And it's the kids who suffer as a result."

A whole lotta rock 'n' roll
Nick Kent, December 23 1972

It's way past the midnight hour and the room at the Angel Hotel, Cardiff, is starting to look a trifle the worse for wear since the motley entourage of Led Zeppelin - "a visiting pop group" - had decided to see the wee wee hours through in its carefully cultivated antiseptic surroundings.

Stray bottles of beer, whisky and coke are strewn around the place, while redundant plates which once held sandwiches lie around the floor. This,

dear friends, is big-time rock 'n' roll...

Big money, big reputation, big business.

Those two tough, short-haired guys sitting in the corner aren't there to look picturesque. Oh, no. They're security, and the best at their job as well.

They've just finished working on the Osmonds' tour.

"Now that was different," says one of them adamantly. "With them, it was just young kids, y'know, but here it's more the sort who get...uh...jealous. Y'know?"

In the middle of the room is the toughest customer of them all - Peter Grant, a mountain of a man and Zep's devoted manager from the very beginning.

This is a character no-one messes around with. BUT NO-ONE.

He's been around and learned a few tricks of the trade, but at the same time he was once Gene Vincent's roadie which means he's a genuine rocker, so that's O.K.

Others in the room are Richard Cole, who looks like a pirate, black beard, ear-ring et al, the slight frame of one B.P. Fallon publicist, and Messrs. Page, Plant, Bonham and Jones. All of which proves nothing less than the indisputable fact that rock 'n' roll is on the road again.

While the Faces are carousing around the suburbs in a good-time Bourbon haze, their stablemates from the weightier side of the Metal Zone, Led Zeppelin, are holed up in

the fair capital city of Wales for a two-day extravaganza of pile-driving rock 'n' roll.

Tonight's show has been "average" – no more, no less, which means that the band got the colossal response they've registered as a customary reaction over the last few years, culminating in a mammoth rock'n'roll medley sandwiched between "Whole Lotta Love" and three encores.

The set lasted over 2 hours and was a constant showcase of how dynamics, musical dexterity and sheer drive should be employed when playing hard rock.

By 1 a.m. the band had quite forgotten about it. Page's only remark afterwards concerned the number of guitar strings that had been broken throughout the proceedings.

Led Zeppelin are more popular and better respected than all their heavy bastard children put together, simply because they are the ace band playing this kind of music – and their audiences know it.

Yet how much do you know about Zeppelin beyond what you hear on record?

Sure, we all know the names of the members and the fact that Jimmy Page used to be in the Yardbirds. Otherwise the Zep Charisma exists almost solely in the music and the band's on-stage persona.

We all know Page, now out-front more than ever, the intense rocker playing the definitive heavy rock guitar; John Paul Jones always in the background; "Bonzo" Bonham thrashing his kit and, out in the spotlight, Robert Plant the precocious lemon-squeezer himself.

Nowadays, when an audience goes to see the Stones it is largely to wallow in the enormous mystique the band has been parading before all of us out here in Mediaville over the years.

With Zeppelin it's the music and rock 'n' roll spectacle that takes precedence every time.

The people come to hear "Whole Lotta Love" or "Stairway to Heaven" or "Dazed and Confused".

You name it, the Zeps will usually always do it and what's more, improve on the studio version.

Offstage the band seem to take on different personalities. Plant abandons his hip-shaking narcissicism to become just one of the lads again.

Bedecked in luxurious Little Lord Fauntleroy golden curls, yokel velvet smock with loose-fitting jacket and jeans, Plant looks more in keeping with the renaissance ballader syndrome until you see the rock 'n' roll-star-beat-up-snake-skin boots on his feet.

He's just returned from a failed attempt to repair the magnificent white elephant of a car he'd just purchased, but is still enthusing about whatever comes to mind.

Mainly, it's music. Buffalo Springfield, the Incredible String Band, Love, Bob Dylan, Elvis Presley, Gene Vincent, Robet Plant's tastes knoweth no boundaries.

"'Forever Changes'. Now there was a great album. Have you heard 'White dog' on 'Vindica-

tor' (Arthur Lee, ex-Love's solo album)? Lee dedicated that for me, y'know.

"He just couldn't believe that I dug his stuff, so much so that he wrote the song."

Someone mentions the name Bob Dylan and Plant is off again.

"Those first two albums - (signs of disbelief and sings a few tentative words to 'Boots of Spanish Leather') - I reckon it was these that brought me round to marijuana.

Plant, a good hippy boy if ever there was one, spends his non-rocking hours close to soil, farming the land, as does drummer Bonham, another bluff son of Birmingham.

The conversation next touches upon such bizarre incidents as the time Page and Plant were lead on an officially conducted tour around the brothels of Thailand.

"We were taken by this guy who spoke strictly Queen's English, y'know, and it seemed to be the policy to show all visiting rock bands the brothels. I mean, it was interesting and that (laughs) but they couldn't understand why we didn't want to do anything.

"The guy kept saying that all the other bands he'd taken round had enjoyed themselves. Eventually we were labelled as undesirables or something because we hadn't got involved. Anyway it's illegal to have long-hair in that country so..."

The scene changes to Texas where Plant was once cornered by the Children of God in an attempt at some sort of conversion.

"It was unbelievably heavy. I mean, they never give up. The first thing they actually said was, would you believe this, 'We've got Jeremy Spencer'!"

Back to the music, Plant talked about lyric-writing.

"It's a shame that the whole solo singer-songwriter concept had to degenerate into that James Taylor thing of taking things so seriously. Actually there are a lot of good ideas going around now.

"Actually this'll probably sound strange, but ultimately I can envisage Pagey and myself end-

Left and right

Bonham and Page caught

live on Zeppelin last ever full

UK Tour, winter 1972/3.

By now, the group needed

no support act – the

evenings were pure 'Led

Zeppelin'

ing-up doing a whole Incredible String Band-type thing together. Very gentle stuff."

Jimmy Page, who looks as if he could still be 20 years old, looks even more rustic-influenced than Plant. His beard has now been sheared while hair has been cut to above shoulder length.

Tonight's stage costume of a black velvet rhinestone jacket has been concealed under Page's obligatory Farmer Giles tweed coat, complete with elbow patches to add final touches of

pastoral simplicity.

Page is one of the rock world's more articulate speakers, though there has yet to appear a definitive piece framed around his words of wisdom. Had this anything to do with the known Zeppelin "Rolling Stone" (the magazine not the rock band) feud from way back when?

"Well, the situation we found ourselves in with 'Rolling Stone' was purely political and stemmed from their side all along. The reasons are basically so trivial that it's really not worth going into."

How did Page feel about journalists' concern with the guitarist's past achievements in rock 'n' roll?

"Everyone seems to ask me about my days with the Yardbirds, which I suppose is

flattering but rather unnecessary, I think."

He also hedges away from talking about his now legendary work as a session musician between 1963-'66, as if bored with bringing up old details.

"It was pretty much uninteresting work, a lot of which has been made more of than it should."

On the development of Zep's albums he had this to say.

"The changes from album to album were these. The first record was made in roughly 30

hours. We went in with some riffs and worked out a set of tracks which were functional as to the sound we were looking for, things we could get off on playing, live.

"The second was recorded in between a lengthy series of gigs we were playing in the States and so obviously the album was affected thus.

"The third album was again affected by a change of pace in that we wrote a number of the songs in Wales and there were various sorts of developments then.

"And the fourth was generally more laid-back in the way it was recorded. It's quite pointless saying 'Oh yeah, this is Led Zeppelin Acoustic Album and this is the Led Zeppelin Heavy Album' because there have been those elements in our music all along and we've never swamped an album with one particular style.

"People claimed that the fourth album was traditionally influenced, but then "Babe I'm Gonna Leave You" is a traditional song and that was the first album."

And about the occasional murmers from certain aficionados that the band have been too concerned with pandering to the tastes of our cousins on the other side of the Atlantic, Page had this to say.

"It's complete rubbish that we concentrate our attentions on the States. If people could be bothered to examine just how much time we do spend in one country at a time you'll find that we measure our touring schedule to take in as many countries as we can.

"This tour of Britain is no less than the tour we did of the States this year. We tried to play around as many countries as possible and everyone ended up saying 'Oh they're ignoring us,' which is rubbish."

Hail Hail Rock 'n' Roll

Nick Kent on the Zeppelin spectacular December 30 1972

There have been two or three truly magic gigs - umm - Bath was one of them.

"That was quite incredible because everything seemed to be right for us. The energy there was quite phenomenal."

Jimmy Page is talking about the Led Zeppelin concert experience.

"Our gigs usually work up out to last around 2 to three hours. I think the longest we ever played was 4 hours, which was another of those magic occasions.

"It was never really a conscious thing that we'd play for so long, it was a gradual process of building up material.

"Someone would want to play this and someone else would throw in a suggestion and eventually we had all this material, both electric and acoustic.

"And then there were the numbers like 'Dazed and Confused' and 'Whole Lotta Love' which come out different every time."

No one introduces Led Zeppelin to the hordes, before they come on. There are never any warm-up acts either: the blinding mass of electronic equipment littering the stage is statement enough of what is about to occur.

The audience have all washed their hair and look eager enough so...it's one for the money two for the show, three to get ready, now...

The band saunter on. Page, dressed in black and looking majestically evil, plugs in while Plant displays his definitive pretty-boy English rock'n'roll star looks and physique under the main spotlight for the first time.

He stands there for a second, looking breathtakingly possessed by the spirit of early Gene Vincent and then, no messing around, Page hits the first power chords of "Rock And Roll" with perfection.

The rock ritual has begun and we're all away. Tonight there are going to be no spectators. And what a song. Recorded in less than 15 minutes for "Led Zeppelin 4" it burns up the first few minutes splendidly and before you can discover what hit you, the band drive on into "Black Dog", which must stand as the ultimate Led Zeppelin heavy riff number, beating even the Plant orang-utang histrionics of "Whole Lotta Love."

God, but it's so brash that it works as perfect rock 'n' roll, never for a moment sounding bland or lacklustre.

Plant never overpowers the stage - he picks his spot and drives the song home with that shrieking voice of his taking deadly aim. The big surprise of this tour, though, is Page, who's up and rockin' alongside the Lemon Squeeze Kid.

While Plant tends to move in curves with the emphasis on the hips, Page seems more deranged, doing knee-bends, thrusting out and using the guitar-neck as a bayonet. He even moves like a demon when playing his weighty twin-neck guitar, flashing weird evil grins when the moods takes him.

But he never leaves one in any doubt that he is total master of his axe.

He never lets up, soldiering his guitar to the rhythm section of Bonham's thrashing and Jones' fine bass to one finely wrought metallic sound.

On "Misty Mountain Hop" he provides the dynamics for Plant to bounce his vocals off, beating out that tricky time signature, and then straight into "Since I've Been Lovin' You," the obligatory blues number.

It's around this time that you realise that the Zep are the ace heavy band.

For a start, they play music and they're - wait for it -tasteful about it. The acoustic set finds Plant and Page seated for "Bron-y-aur Stomp" and another number which makes this the shortest non-electric sequence the band have done.

Actually, the band's real peaks come when they play their gentler compositions electrically to hold the dynamics together more effectively.

A new composition "The Song Remains The Same" drives on with Page mingling major and minor chords to dazzling effect and Bonham thrashing his kit with a vengence.

The song sounds almost like Yes in construction, with the emphasis on the dexterity of rock 'n' roll, and then the song breaks to accommdoate a luxurious Page chord passage which heralds the performance of "Rain Song", another newie.

By the end of the number - a "Stairway to Heaven" type of epic work - the band sound like a full-blown orchestra.

Next up is "Dancing Days", the third introduction to the fifth Led Zeppelin album repertoire, this time an unselfconscious rocker celebrating school holidays and general teenage liberation, packing some of the bland aspects to be found in Alice Cooper's self-styled anthem "School's Out".

Below

Robert Plant – Light and

Shade

Overleaf

Live Led

Plant oohs and aahs through the vocals, leaving the show to Page and his magic violin bow. Many eerie futuristic scraping sounds are emitted from the guitar and the number is climaxed by Page slapping the bow against the strings to spectacular effect and pointing the bow at the audience evil-magician style.

To prove their point the Zeps pull the ace from their sleeve and go into the introduction of "Stairway to Heaven", which must be the band's finest musical achievement.

Then the song starts to take a majestic shape, sailing on until it breaks loose into the final part with everyone giving the final gasp as Plant sings "To Be A Rock and Not To Roll". Supreme live experience rock 'n' roll.

Well what can a poor boy do now but drive on into another golden oldie.

No more Lemon Squeezing, so it's time for what must be thè chrominium-plated heavy rocker of the '60s, sharing the title with "Louie, Louie" by the Kingsmen - "Whole Lotta Love."

Now here is a pulp classic if ever there was - inane as they come, and directly influenced by the Small Faces "You Need Love" which was in turn influenced by...well, you name it...and it's classic punk rock.

The band barnstorm straight through it, stopping just before the end to go into a medley of good ole' rock 'n roll.

Anything can be performed in the inimitable Zep style at this juncture of the proceedings and to make no bones about it, the band show they mean business by kicking off with "Blue Suede Shoes".

From there it's anyone's guess, but it's "Let's Have A Party" - "Some People like to rock...Some people like to roll."

You must know all about it. A few tentative verses of "Let The Boy Rock 'N' Roll" follow, to be capped with a merciless rendition of "Bee-Bop-a-Lula" which has Plant doing his best Vincent impersonation.

It's one more verse of "Whole Lotta Love" and then off to be followed by three separte encores, first "Heartbreaker", second a new song called "The Ocean".

"This is about you" says Plant, matter-of-factly to the audience, and finally, a long version of "Thank You" with John Paul Jones excelling on mellotron.

Outside the hall, the inevitable bunch of young kids, mostly male, babble on excitedly about the concert.

"I mean...like, I saw Emerson, Lake and Palmer two weeks ago...and, like, they're good musicians and all...but Led Zeppelin...y'know."

We all know. Hail, Hail Rock 'n Roll.

Houses of the Holy

The delayed fifth album, Houses Of The Holy, was finally released in March. Like Led Zeppelin III, it suffered something of a mauling from critics who found its pot-pourri of different styles unsettling - which did not stop it hitting No.1 on both sides of the Atlantic. The year was dominated by the band's biggest-ever US tour, which saw them flying between the 37 dates by private airliner, and included several shows to audiences bigger than 50,000. The final gigs at Madison Square Garden, New York, were filmed by director Joe Massot for use in a projected Led Zeppelin movie, and when the band returned to the UK in the Autumn, each member (including manager Peter Grant) also filmed an individual sequence - essentially a fantasy piece of their own choice - with Massot, for use in the film. In the event, the movie would be several years in somewhat difficult gestation.

Zep make masochism worthwhile

Roy Carr March/April, 1973

Led Zeppelin: "Houses Of The Holy" (Atlantic). There's a masochistic pleasure that comes with every new Led Zeppelin album...the waiting.

I don't think any of us really appreciate just how many midnight candles are burned to produce an album of the highest possible quality. And there are few bands as meticulous as the Zeppites over their craft.

With a quick burst of six-string machine-gun fire supported by bass and percussion artillery, the intro to "The Song Remains The Same" is extended to accommodate Magic Jimmy's slashed guitar chords prior to the tempo being halved and Robert P. Zeppelin boppin' up to the mike to moan in his best Lucy In The Skies voice (slightly speeded up 'n' phased), "I had a dream-crazy dream".

Thereafter he offers verbal imagery of California sunlight, sweet Calcutta rain, Honolulu starlight, sings Hare hare and invites one and all to dance the Hoochie Koo.

In every song that ensues, Page's dexterity extracts just about everything that can be extracted from a guitar, and then for an encore some things that can't.

For "The Rain Song", acoustic guitars extend the direction first premiered on "Stairway to Heaven" and "California". Plantey gets his best ballad chops working on this one, and John Paul Jones creates the Zeppelin Symphony Orchestra on Mellotron. Very pastoral and beefed up towards the end, with some well-timed dynamics.

Far Left

JPJ displays keyboard wizardry

Left

Robert Plant wows 'em

This same mood is virtually retained intact for "Over the Hills And Far Away". To cushion the undoctored vocal track, Page supplements his acoustic playing with a secondary electric line, and then when Bonzo and John Paul Jones chug along in familiar style he adds a third guitar to growl out a hot and nasty solo.

Good Gawd y'all. Are yer feelin' alright? Well it's showtime, so get on the good foot, 'cause Pagey's got a brand-new bag and do the Funky Zeppelin, or to be more precise "The Crunge" with Mr. James P. Led & his Lemon Squeezin' Soul Brothers. Right On. Right On. Right On.

With Bonzo Bonham the destructor poundin' out a grits and greens 9/4 back-beat, Page punctuates the rhythm with clipped guitar licks as Brother Bobby shows James Brown where it's currently at.

Somewhere along the way J.P. 'Hogfat' Jones supplies the brass parts via synthesiser to close side one.

"Dancing Days" proved a crowd pleaser when incorporated into the recent Led Zep Road Show. On wax it's just as good, with some unusual chord progressions and a strong vocal lead from the guv'nor. The lad just gets better and better with each outing.

With each album Led Zeppelin break new ground, and as Toots Page and his Ras Rude Boys they produce some heavy metal reggae on 'D'yer Maker'. Let's face it, like everything the band attempt, it's a bloody marvellous track with a fine workout from Bonzo. It just shows you what a diet of bananas and best bitter can do.

Yet another musical depature is revealed in "No Quarter", with all four gentlemen producing an extrememly ethereal mood which pivots around some super-slick piano - grand and synthesised - from J.P. Jones. Another faultless track which I'm sure points a direction for things to come.

For a flag-waving closer, Bonham gets up to his tricks again to lay down a thundering 7/4 beat, split up into one bar of three every three bars of four. I don't pretend to be Ian Mcfalable (it's RC not RW), but I won't spoil your fun, I'll leave that up to you to figure out.

But please note, proceed with the utmost caution when either clappin' or dancin' along. This is the kinda music that helped Zep conquer the world, and it benefits from perhaps the greatest live-in-the-studio sound I've heard in yonks.

Just before the end, bouncing Bobby yells out "So Good" - a built-in do-it-yourself-review. So who am I to argue.

Vive le Zeppelin

Roy Hollingworth reports from Paris April 7th, 1973

"I'm back on me fab farm like and I sit there and I think what the hell am I doing? I think what the bloody hell is a singer if he's not singing?" says Robert Plant.

We're surrounded by last night's champagne corks, wall-to-wall tapestries and sweaty socks. We're here at the George V hotel, lavish as you like, where everything from your pillow to the toilet seat bears the hotel's legendary monogram.

Bleating

Plant lies sprawled across my bed bleating endlessly about the finesse of Wolverhampton Wanderers and Led Zeppelin - something he believes in like nobody has ever believed in anything ever before.

It rains chats and chiens outside, mid-morning, dark and windy.

The clouds are full of menace - as were Zeppelin last night. They kicked a great hole in the night, splitting it all open down at the city's massive Palais des Sportes stadium where they finished their European tour.

"So there's some buggers 'as don't like the album. Well, God bless them. I like it and there's a few thousand other buggers like it too. I know I'm bragging like buggery but I henestly think we're playing better than we've ever played before."

"It's working that does it. The British tour three weeks off, and then a solid blow over here. It's so easy to get stale, you know.

Peak

"There's a lot of bands do it. You know they reach a peak and think that that's it. The old country house bit. A year off and all that.

"Well, it doesn't work that way. There's only one way a band can function and that's on the bloody stage. I think we're going to play more dates this year than we've ever played in our lives. Why? Well, because we damn well want to."

"I remember a few weeks back, sat on me farm. Well, it came to me, I thought 'Plantey, what's a good lad like you doing sat here contemplating the day like an old goat?'

"I thought why the ... ain't I out singing. I got so worked up about it that I picked up a spade and dug the whole bloody garden. I have to work, we all have to."

Despite this chirpiness Plant is like all of Zeppelin - ultra-sensitive. When it comes down to criticising them, you might as well forget it. It's rather like telling the Pope that there ain't no God, if you see what I mean.

You see, Zeppelin can be a heavy bunch of lads at times, but we won't go into that.

At Heathrow, we sat waiting for the Paris flight complete with *Sunday Mirrors* and early morning sickness. Meanwhile the rest of England prepared itself for Sunday lunches and cozy BBC wireless messages from BFPO service adresses in Bahrain ("Hello Jean").

We decided to drink brandy. It was at the Heathrow bar that we met Fat Fred and Patsy who between them offer the good thirty stones of chirpy cockney music.

Heavies

Now Fat Fred and Patsy are professional heavies. They are hired as bodyguards by rock groups. It's no show of amateur dramatics for Patsy was sporting a good twelve stitches in his chest following a Zeppelin gig in Northern Europe.

They'd left the band in Southern France after a ridiculous night which saw most of the group and road crew end up in the local jail.

Far Left, Top

'Bonjour Paris'

Far Left, Below

Bonham 'Moby Dick', USA 1973

Above

Page – 'Blinded by the Lights', USA 1973

"But the fuzz was petrified of us," said Patsy. "We was so wild that they decided to let us go before we dismantled the prison.

"Give us a mention, I mean the lads who look after David Cassidy are bleeding superstars now."

Well, Zeppelin conquered again last night. They turned an audience that resembled dumb figures at the start into a terrifying mass of hysteria.

There's Bonzo Bonham, this Desperate Dan of a character thrashing and splatting his way into the night and Pagey darting across the stage, snitching chords clean, quick and loud. It's all so urgent.

Roar

"When I hear that roar I just roar back. I can't describe how high we get off people," said Plantey.

They played very well, did Zeppelin. Solid slogging work that has now brought about total live perfection.

I've said it before - their ability to reach an impeccable high and sustain it for three hours is an astonishing feat.

"Yeah, we have reached a high," said Plant, "and we ain't going to lose it.

"And no lousy album review is going to change a thing."

Zeppin' Out

Charles Shaar Murray reports from Los Angeles, June 16 1973

"I don't even like Led Zeppelin." the girl in the black velvet jacket and hotpants said petulantly as

she bummed a cigarette off an acquaintance in the lobby of the Continental Hyatt House Hotel in L.A. "I'm only staying here because my friends have a room. I think Zep are really tacky."

This particular lady's name was Sherry. Despite her olive skin and California tan, her face proudly bore the scars of pimples galore. Nice legs though. Anyway, she and her friends had the signal honour of being personally evicted from Zep's floor by no less than Robert Plant himself. Plant has no patience with groupies these days.

So with no further ado, let us adjourn to the Forum in L.A. It is May 31, and the time is eight o'clock on a Thursday night.

One of the first things one notices about Zeppelin's audiences is their calm and serenity. Two nights before I'd seen Humble Pie play Madison Square Garden in New York, and for the first time in many years of concert going, I was glad to have a policeman standing next to me. The Pie crowd were so out of their collective mind on red wine and quaaludes that a nasty incident seemed imminent at any time.

Not so with the Zep crowd. They got their rocks off all right, and they shook and twitched till they were as sweaty and exhausted as the band, but not once did anybody give off a violent vibe. For all its enormous volume and energy, Zeppelin's music is inappropriate music to split skulls to.

So all is in readiness. Suddenly the lights explode, and there they are. John Paul Jones with shortish hair, moustache and five-string bass, looking almost as if he'd just

Previous Page

Studies of Jimmy Page (top),

Robert Plant (Below)

Right

Bonham lays down the beat

Below

'Whole Lotta Love'

Far right, top

'Full frontal assault'

Below

Jones and Page relax backstage,

post-gig, January 1973

left the Eagles, Page bare-chested in black velvets sparingly sequinned, carrying a business-like Les Paul, Bonham settling in behind his kit to check it out, and leonine Robert Plant in flowered shirt and jeans. The opening number is "Rock And Roll".

Where Zeppelin score over all the bands who've come up in their wake and endeavoured to emulate them is that they keep all the bases covered. Everything that's part of the show is meticulously polished until it's as good as it can possibly get. Nothing sags, nothing is second-rate, nothing is skimped.

Every arrangement, every improvisation, the construction of every song or every solo - nothing is neglected. It's simply good traditional British craftsmanship. The word "sloppy" is, for all practical purposes, not part of Led Zeppelin's collective vocabulary.

On the other hand, it's certainly no sterile rehearsed-into-the-ground Yes trip, because each gig has as much excitement and freshness and enthusiasm as if it

was their first and last.

Generally, the length of a band's set gives you some idea how much they enjoy playing together. Zeppelin play between two and three hours. Enough said.

The L.A. Forum gig was pretty damn good. It blew me out completely, but it was to be completely dwarfed in my memory by the San Francisco date they played two days later. So on with the show.

Backstage, the hangers-on have moved in and commenced to hang on. Fourteen-year-old girls in cheap gaudy threads are wandering about disconsolately muttering, "Where's Jimmy?", bumming dimes for the chewing gum machine, surreptitiously flashing their photo spreads in *Star* magazine, and hectoring photographers into taking their pictures.

Lee Childers from Mainman's L.A. office is there in a white suit, taking pictures of everything in sight.

"What's this," he asks, "in some of the English papers about me and Cherry getting fired? All that happened was that we went back home to look after our offices. Why do people print things they know aren't true?" He seems quite upset, as well he might be.

In the corner, Robert Plant is leaning against a wall drinking beer. He's changed into a rhinestone Elvis T-shirt, and he is lavish in his praise of the audience. "What a beautiful buzz," he keeps saying. "If it wasn't for Jimmy's hand, we could've played all night for those people. Weren't they great?", he asks everybody within reach.

Jump cut to the party scene. It's John Bonham's birthday, and the Forum audience had given him a hero's tribute for his drum marathon on "Moby Dick" earlier in the evening. "Twenty-one today," as Plant had announced from the stage.

"This party is probably going to get very silly," he announces. Why else would a man turn up to his birthday party wearing a T-shirt, plimpsols and a pair of swimming trunks? As things turn out, he was probably the most appropriately clad person present.

The party is at the luxurious Laurel Canyon home of a gentleman who runs a radio station, and to prove his importance, he discreetly displays photographs of himself with such disparate notables as Sly Stone and Richard (the man from W.A.T.E.R.G.A.T.E) Nixon.

Having flown in from Louisiana that morning, your reporter disgraces himself by falling asleep in a chair at around 4.30a.m. A little later, he is

awakened by the very considerate Phil Carson from Atlantic Records and returned, more or less in one piece, to his hotel.

Next day he learns that virtually everyone present ended up in the pool after George Harrison hit Bonzo

with his own birthday cake. Mr. Fallon's antique velvet costume was totalled by his immersion, as was Rodney Bingeneimer's camera and a mink coat belonging to a lady named Vanessa.over the rest of the proceedings we will draw a slightly damp veil.

Saturday and San Francisco. Jimmy Page is paranoid about flying in Zep's small private jet, so he and manager Peter Grant are travelling on a scheduled flight.

That leaves Plant, Bonzo, JPJ, Beep, Peter Grant's deputy Richard Cole (who I first met some years ago in a Reading labour exchange) and sundry others to brave the elements in this tiny craft.

The chicken and champagne help to ease the terrors, except for one moment when the indefatigable Mr. Bonham pilots the plane. Luckily, I don't find out about that until he's back in his seat.

The gig is open-air, in a stadium at Golden Gate Park. Zep have been preceded by Lee Michaels, Roy Harper and a local group called Tubes. Harper is reported to have silenced hecklers by informing them that "Zeppelin haven't even left L.A. yet, so fuckin' shut up."

In the backstage area, Bill Graham is prowling around checking people out for passes. Bonham mutters something about having a hard time playing in the intense heat, but luckily it gets cooler later on. In the crowd, a black policeman is wearing an "Impeach Nixon" badge. San Francisco still has a lot of soul.

Above

'The Song Remains The Same'–

a Zeppelin tour-de-force

Below

Classic Bonham

Right

'In Complete Vision'

Quite unselfconsciously, quite unobtrusively any place they play becomes a House Of The Holy, a place to straighten tangled brain cells. Simultaneously, they take you right back to your rock and roll home, and send you to some new places that already feel like home when you arrive. A very spiritual occasion indeed, and also a very physical moment.

And despite all the disillusionment, the San Francisco dream is not over. It's just that nowadays people just don't talk about it. In that park, everything seemed cleaner, fresher and somehow more immediate.

For me, one of the most amazing moments of the whole show was, strangely enough, the part I expected to enjoy least. All my musical life I've had a strong antipathy towards drum solos. Thus, it came as a shock to find myself really getting off on Bonzo's "Moby Dick".

How can I tell you about that show? Led Zeppelin and 50,000 San Francisco people got together to provide one of the finest musical events I've ever had the privilege to attend. There may be bands who play better, and there may be bands who perform better, and there may be bands who write better songs, but when it comes to welding themselves and their audience together into one solid unit of total joy, Zeppelin yield to nobody.

Whether they're punching out the riffs of "Black Dog", or stealing people's hearts from the inside them with "Stairway to Heaven" (as far as I'm concerned Zeppelin's all-time masterpiece) or tripping the audience out with those unbelievable Plant-Page guitar/vocal call-and-response set pieces, they just transmit magic to anybody within hearing range.

Watching him from a few feet away, totally absorbed in what he was doing, it came back to the craftsmanship thing again. He didn't look, as so many endlessly soloing drummers do, as if they're playing to the gallery. He resembled nothing so much as a sculptor or a painter or anybody who's doing anything which involves concentration, effort and skill.

John Bonham was plying his trade, doing his gig, exercising his own particular skills, doing what any gifted and committed craftsman does. It's always nice to break through

a prejudice and dig something that you couldn't dig before.

Altogether, a magical concert. I suppose legions of die-hard Zep freaks have known this all along, but for me it was a revelation. Throughout the solo, Plant was pacing the side of the stage, occasionally swinging himself up the scaffolding to sit under the amps. "Do you feel it?", he said. "Feel that buzz!"

After "Communication Breakdown" a water fight broke out backstage, and about the only person who escaped unscathed was promoter Bill Graham. Zeppelin went back out to do a final encore of "The Ocean", and then made a dash for the limos.

All hail, Led Zep. Hosannas by the gram. If there's any excitement still left in this ego circus we call rock and roll, a sizeable portion of it derives from you. Be proud.

Robert Plant - and that below-the-belt surge

From LA, an exclusive interview

by Charles Shaar Murray, June 23 1973

A hot and sticky Friday afternoon in L.A. Nine storeys over Sunset Boulevard, Robert Plant takes Roy Harper's "Lifemask" off the stereo in his hotel room and sprawls all over one of the beds. He's wearing a pair of leather jeans and little else, and he's sweating fairly profusely.

Why would a happy family man with a lovely wife, child and farm voluntarily rush all over the world putting himself through all the major and minor dramas of touring?

"This is a very close, tightly knit, sensitive group, one member to the next. We've got a very strong bond, and so working is a pleasure.

"What happened was that, after we made the third album, Jimmy and I were in Wales and we were fed up with going to America. We'd been going twice a year, and at that time America was really a trial, an effort.

"Anyway, we didn't work for a year, and we said to ouselves: 'Look, this is terrible, let's get going, let's move.' So in the past year we've played every single market that a band in our position could possibly play." .

In Plant's eyes, their musical strong point is the ability to be able to tackle something like "D'Yer Maker" - "Desmond Dekker meets Led Zeppelin" - and hold their credibility. "This is the finest property we possess - without it, the group would be a bore. Not naming names, there are a lot of groups in England who still rely on riff after riff after riff.

"Some audiences can shake and bang their heads on the stage to riffs all night long, but subtlety is an art that must be mastered if you're to be remembered.

"In this band we're very lucky that everybody is more enthusiastic as time goes on. There is not fatigue or boredom musically at all. There's a bit of boredom when you're stuck in Mobile, Alabama, or places like that. A few lamp standards may fall out of the windows - things like that - but we move on and we keep playing that music.

"It's just this rapport that we've got between ourselves. It's a good buzz. Man, I mean, I've learned how to feel an audience now, and that's my success. I can feel them, they can feel me. If you can't you're not doing anything at all.

"There are a lot of groups who come over here and play very loud and very monotonously and get people off...but, the other way, it's almost like putting your hands out and touching everybody. That's probably why we're coming back here in three weeks.

"You see, my little boy's just started to walk, and I haven't seen him bloomin' walk yet. Those are the things that upset you about being on the road. The very fact that you miss fantastic occasions like that.

"I mean, the kid just stands up and starts strolling around – and here I am in Tuskaloosa or wherever."

Is is not practical for you to take your family on the road?

"Oh, it'd be chaotic for a young kid. I don't like taking Maureen either really, as much as I love her. When you are on the road, you are nomads, you know. There was an album called 'Rock 'n' Roll Gypsies' and that's it - you've gotta travel on.

"Robert Johnson once said: 'Woke up this morning /got the rain off my shoes/my woman left me/got the walking blues.' It's just great to move on and set up in another town and see the people there smiling.

"I think I've got one of the finest ladies in the world and it wouldn't do her any good because she's not up there on that stage. So she'd get tired and want to know why we weren't doing this and that, and the very fact that I've just woken up and

it's three o'clock in the afternoon and the shops shut at six, and there's no shopping to be done today and all that sort of thing...It isn't practical."

One of the most admirable things about Zeppelin in recent times has been the atmosphere of Celtic mysticism that has seeped into some of the songs. "Stairway to Heaven" is of course the classic example, with its allusions to various Cornish and Welsh myths.

"That was present really from the second album onwards," says Plant when drawn on the subject. "It was something that we did well, and was pointing in a specific direction. Then there was 'Ramble On', 'Thank You', 'Going To California', 'The Battle Of Evermore', 'The Rain Song' - on the new album too - even 'The Song Remains The Same'.

"Every time I sing that, I just picture the fact that I've been round and round the world, and at the root of it all there's a common denominator for everybody. The common denominator is what makes it good or bad, whether it's a Led Zeppelin or an Alice Cooper.

"The lyrics I'm proud of. Somebody pushed my pen for me, I think.

"There are a lot of catalysts which really bring out those sort of things: working with the group, living where I live, having the friends I've got, my children, my animals.

"There's also the fact that people have finally come to terms with the fact that, three years ago, we made a classic record with 'Whole Lotta Love', and they realise that it's just one colour in the rainbow of what we do and what we are intending to

do in the future.

"I think we've got a lot of friends in England. I remember Bradford on the last tour, when the audience were superb.

"'Stairway to Heaven' gets the best reaction of any number we do. But the raunchiness is in everybody: that below-the-belt surge that everybody gets at some time or another.

"Everybody gets their rocks off, I suppose, and we supply a little bit of music to that end."

In the last eight months Zeppelin have been literally working solid. "We were going back and forward to America, and then to Japan, Hong Kong

and Bangkok.

"Jimmy and I did some recording in India with the Bombay Symphony Orchestra. It was an experiment, and we know what we want to do next time."

Hmmmm. Are they likely to be releasing any

Far Left, in circle

Plant in full flight onstage

Far Left, Below

'Waiting for the Starship'

Below

John Paul Jones, 'No Quarter'

Jimmy Page, the enigma of the band. Offstage, a polite, soft spoken and almost gentleman-like figure. Onstage, a human dynamo fuelling the fire and always pushing the band to new great heights

of that material?

"Not those, no. We were just checking out, just sussing how easy it would be to transpose the ideas that we've got into the raga style, and into the Indian musicians' minds.

"It's very hard for them to cope with the Western approach to music with their counting of everything, their times and so on.

"Where we count four beats to the bar, their bars just carry on and on. They'll be counting up to 99 or 100, and on the 120th boomph you change, instead of on the 18th bar or something like that. But anyway, we found that whatever we might want to play, we can do successfully in time to come.

"We moved on from there and played Switzerland, Scandinavia, Germany and France.

"Promotion people are absolutely nuts over there, and the kids are more interested in using a concert as an excuse to be leery, most of the time.

I don't really like that. I don't consider that I've gained anything when I see that there's a lot of fools fighting.

"The gig you saw last night was a magic one because the people were so relaxed. It was as if I'd known them years.

"The vibe that we give out could never advocate or encourage violence. A fight in there would have been totally contradictory to the whole vibe of the place, and everybody would have been totally disgusted."

"You've got to have a rapport with the people, and that rapport must eradicate any feelings like that. Alice Cooper's weirdnesses must really make the kids feel violent. These kids are like my sister, young people of 14 or so who've come to enjoy themselves. So you put things like that in front of them, and I don't think it's right.

"My idea is that I should go on stage and be completely normal, and it pays. It pays immensely because I get that vibe right back. That's the thesis really, that's the reason for our success here."

Zeppelin are one band who it's bad for your head to miss. What is it that does that? Is it the chemistry of the four people?

"Yeah, it's the desire to really want to lay something down for ever and ever and ever. I would like to create something now, and be part of the creation of something now, that would be valid for years and years to come. Not so much in the way that Chuck Berry will be valid in 50 years time, which he will, but something like a mammoth stairway which takes in a lot of the mood of the group.

It's my ambition to write something really superb. I listen a lot to people like Mendelssohn – and it's absolutely superb. You can picture exactly where that guy was. You can picture the whole thing and I'd like it to be the same way for us in time to come. Last night, when all those lights were there, that was a kind of spiritual allegiance. You walk out there and they're going, 'Yea, we know you can do it' - and with that sort of thing tucked inside your belt you can only go from strength to strength.

"Somebody once described me as the original hippie and that's because of the flowery lyrics, you know, and also because of the buzz we give out."

The onstage energy of Led Zeppelin. Each member of the band grew to know, almost instinctively, how the other members were thinking. Much improvisation resulted from this relationship and some numbers were rarely performed the same twice

Swan Song Debut

This year, in partnership with Atlantic, the band launched in May their own Swan Song record label (a name that grew from a title which Jimmy Page had given to an in-progress musical track), which signed Bad Company, Maggie Bell and the Pretty Things, as well as releasing Led Zeppelin's own records from here on. Otherwise, in contrast to the frenzied touring of 1973, this was to be a quieter 12 months for the band, during which their next album slowly but surely took shape. The projected movie, however, temporarily ground to a halt, with Zeppelin splitting (due to differences over "priorities") from Joe Massot, who had directed all the footage to date, and installing rock documentary film-maker Peter Clifton in his place. It would be a further two years before the world was to see and hear the final result. The band's riotous October 31 Hallowe'en party at Chislehurst Caves in Kent was, however, the rock social event of the year, becoming legendary in its excesses.

The man who led Zeppelin

With a background in wrestling, it's not surprising that Peter Grant is cast as heavy. An exclusive interview with Michael Watts June 22, 1974

NEWSFLASH: Atlantic Records has signed the hot new English group, Led Zeppelin, to a long-term, exclusive recording contract. Although the exact terms of the deal are secret, it can be disclosed that it is one of the most substantial deals Atlantic has ever made. Agreement for the group's services was made between Jerry Wexler, Executive Vice-President of Atlantic Records, and Peter Grant, manager of the group...

The stories, of course, are legion, and have become pop myths with the passage of time. Stories of sexual excess, of physical devastation, of huge sums made (and stolen), of elaborate and somewhat cruel practical joking, and of acts of what might vulgarly be described as "heaviness."

How, for instance, the frustrated assistant manager of a hotel in Seattle was gifted by said group with a room in his own establishment to smash up, all in the cause of tension relief, expenses paid; how a stoned PR man awoke at dead of night to find a pony and chickens in his room; or how the London king of the bootlegs was "paid a visit," during which he was relieved of his six quid Zeppelin pirates.

And Frank Zappa, it should be recalled, used to have a tale about the sexual utilisation of the mudshark fish.

None of it apocrypha. Not those, at any rate, which Peter Grant tells. If he says so, who then is inclined to disbelieve?

For truly he is a man whose reputation precedes him, a man afforded great respect by his peers, and without feeling of respect what is there to distinguish men from beasts?

Called to the defence, indeed, Tony Stratton-Smith, a friend as well as pop manager of some eloquence, will testify that Grant "is a model professional in management."

And when pressed, that he's "a fighter - tough but straightforward." Indeed.

"So then there was the time," continues Grant, "of the sailors, who were 'aving a go at Jimmy Page and Jeff Beck. The three of us were flying down to Miami, and I turn round and hear these blokes.

"One of 'em looked like a little touch, so I lifted him up under the arm and said 'okay, what's your trouble, Popeye?' The other one ran."

And no wonder. Grant was once known in the wrestling ring as Count Massimo, a fact of history he's anxious to consign to oblivion now that he's a figure of much professional respect.

Unfortunately, it all came out in an interview with the *Daily Mirror* three years ago, and ever since he's held people from "the rags" at arm's length.

But consider the man. Thirty-nine years old, he's in the form of an identikit, B-movie villain thought up by central casting. A large, brawny and fleshy person, equipped with a formidable paunch and a heavily-bearded head that hulks on his shoulders.

In Boys' Own idiom, the adjective would leap forth from the pages as "sinister," "evil-minded," "cruel-eyed" and "ferocious," with the addition of such nouns as "giant," "brute" and "devil."

If he ever wore anything more imposing than his perennial and shabby jeans, a case could be made out for the lead role of Rasputin. As it is, a bodyguard in a Turkish harem seems more appropriate.

It should be stated, in fact, that the theatrical appearance has indeed been capitalised upon in the past, though not with much obvious glory.

He played a cowboy once in a Benny Hill show, and has been in Dixon of Dock Green and a Sid James series. In The Saint he was a barman, and had two lines; his two kids nearly died when that episode was reshown.

And then he doubled for Robert Morley in a movie, although the facial resemblance, if not the comparative stomachs, is slight. He was even a waiter in a mime act starring a fellow called Eddie Vitch: beat that, David Bowie.

"There was a lovely description of me in an American magazine," he will chuckle. "They called me" - he begins to laugh out loud – " 'the ex-rock errand boy.' It was f-great. Fantastic."

Then there is the Grant Voice. As with many big men, the vocal organ turns out to be a remarkably mild instrument albeit prone to the expletive. Not a gruff bark at all, but soft and slow, with a South Norwood twang to it. Still, who needs a second Sidney Greenstreet?

And by the way, he adds in that voice, casually flicking the ash from chain-smoked cigarettes on to his shirt-front, since I seem to know so many stories about him, and Zeppelin, he thinks he'll ring around to dig some about me. It was much nicer than it sounds, somehow.

There's an obvious temptation, however, to play up Peter Grant as an archetypal, one-dimensional heavy, an anachronism from that pop era when businessmen were not necessarily gentlemen, and smooth lawyers, accountants and the oiled machinations of Big Business had not yet arrived in number.

The caricatured appearance heightened the effect of the stories and so, oddly enough, does the knowledge that he lives in a 15th-century manor house in a Sussex village, surrounded by antiques, 65 acres of land, his own stretch of river, bullocks, cows and numerous vintage cars.

Isn't that the life all pop stars and managers retire to once they've made their first pile? (And, in fact, within the vicinity live Keith Emerson, Adam Faith and two of his own group, John Paul Jones and Jimmy Page.)

Well, yes it is, but then Grant seems such a transparent Englishman, in all his John Bull bluntness, that on reflection it's hard to believe he feels the need to show off.

His house is exquisite and tasteful - not a sign of chrome rubbing shoulders with ancient timber.

Doubtless those involved in pop appreciate all the more the permanence and tradition of antique possessions from a realisation of the transience of their own working lives.

Schizophrenia, moreover, is a palpable factor of rock life; mulish behaviour is expected on the road, but p's and q's are watched at home.

Grant takes an obvious delight in his old tapestries and pieces - like the little art deco liqueur decanter Page gave him for Christmas - and the fact that his sparrow-like wife Gloria teaches kids ballet just across the garden there.

But that's home.

"If," he emphasises, "I'm out at a concert and somebody is gonna do something that's snide to one of my artists, then I'll f - tread on 'em without thinking about it."

The more one talks to him, the more apparent it becomes that his bullishness of speech and action go a long way toward explaining his reputation.

He has a fierce dislike of pomp and circumstance, for example, and a positive antipathy to snobs.

He recalls that he was once flying on the Playboy plane with Hugh Hefner, whom he describes, with a slight air of theatrical indifference, as "a bit boring, actually. Not really me. You know, people that've got a lotta bread but still play at being affluent are boring."

Neither does he have much time for jet-set society, a feeling apparently shared by Led Zeppelin. For instance, there was the picture on the front page of that prestigious American magazine, *Women's Wear Daily*, of Mick Jagger and Ahmet Ertegun, president of Atlantic records.

Grant's voice rises in incredulity: emphatic.

"I - cannot - imagine - me - ringing - up Robert - Plant - and saying 'listen, it's you and me, baby. Ahmet Ertegun wants his picture on the front of such-and-such'."

You wouldn't have to use the phone to hear the reply from Wales. You could stand outside the house and hear the scream of hysterics.

"But quite honestly, I wouldn't know what to talk to all those people about, anyway.

"When we were in America recently, launching Swan Song (the new label owned jointly by Grant and Zeppelin), a woman from the *Hollywood Reporter* came up and said, 'I know you're very busy now, but I must call you at the hotel. I'm gonna definitely call you tomorrow to get some interesting facts.'

"And I said, just as a throwaway, 'call me at 12 noon and I'll tell you something boring.' And she swept out of the reception in a great long evening dress."

And he was upset?

A slow smile, "I though it was f - great. I mean, I know some of those bigshots at the record company cringe when they're with me, 'cause I don't even own a suit, just two pairs of jeans."

Leaning back in an armchair he surveys his shirt with a large tear in one sleeve. "But I know

they have to do it because of what you represent. Which is great."

He currently represents Bad Company and Maggie Bell (whom he co-manages with an American named Mark London), as well as Zeppelin, all of whom, he feels, conform to a pattern of being musicianly artists.

The idea of him looking after a lot of tarts in glitter is as absurd as it's problematical; or, to put it his way, he wouldn't know what the f - to do with Sweet:

"I'd be like a fish out of water; it just wouldn't be me. I'd feel uncomfortable, and I would probably f - up for them."

With Maggie Bell, on the contrary, he enjoys what is almost a father-daughter relationship, it's said - a comment that draws from him both surprise and gratification.

He's highly protective of all his artists, but especially sensitive about Ms. Bell and the reason why she hasn't quite made it in Britain yet.

"Don't forget," he expostulates, "that in terms of the relative sizes of each country, she's selling the same amount of records here as in America.

"And you put an advrtisement in your paper for a tour next week and I bet you we sell out within three days!"

The trouble is, he explains, they've yet to hit on the right formula for an album as it was. "Queen Of The Night" had been out with Mark London and Felix Pappalardi before the record was issued with the legendary Jerry Wexler of Atlantic as producer.

"The problem with Felix is that he wanted to use too many of his own songs, his missus being co-writer, and he was using Leslie West too much on it; the whole thing just didn't gel.

"I don't understand music very much, but it's a feel thing: it gives you a tingle, and you know.

"But anyway, Wexler heard some stuff, got on the phone and said, 'Jee-zus Christ!' So I told him: 'your gotta remember that's the f - act you turned down four years ago, yer schmuck'. Still, he was prepared to be magnanimous. And he cut a really nice album.

"But you see, the album lacks balls and it lacks Maggie Bell. You want that magic of her walking out onstage coming out of those speakers - almost her gobbing on you - and it doesn't happen.

"It's too immaculate! Too immaculate. It's just not her."

Now with Zeppelin, of course, it had been instant whammy from the start but only in America. A short tour of Scandinavia as Jimmy Page and the New Yardbirds, a few struggling dates in Great Britain, then the first tour of the States as Led Zeppelin, the four horsemen of the heavy

rock apocalypse.

In America their first album, recorded at Olympic in Britain, was on the Stateside charts at 98 the first week it was released, before they'd even played there.

They did a week with Vanilla Fudge, playing big, seatless halls, and on a couple of dates were so successful that Fudge would go on first.

And when the word got out, a lot of so-called heavy underground American groups were wary of having Zep on the show at all. The band returned to Britain after that first tour and continued to play clubs, until one night Grant drove to Klook's Kleek in Hampstead and there was a queue 300 yards around the block.

Led Zeppelin were essentially the first big band to establish the formula of success-in-America-imitation-in-Britain, which is much more difficult to follow now in America when the opinion-making venues have largely disappeared.

Grant consciously planned it. Having previously toured with the Yardbirds in America he had an insight into the underground scene, and importantly, believed he knew what was the real mood of the country.

Here Zeppelin fought at first against public indifference or active hostility to what some considered a contrivance, a plasticised New Yardbirds.

But a deal was done with Atlantic in New York almost before the band had been formed. Page was well-known at the label, not merely because of his bass-playing with the Yardbirds, but also through his work with Bert Burns.

And Dusty Springfield had told Jerry Wexler a lot about John Paul Jones, with whom she'd done sessions in Britain.

Grant had initially been involved during the period when he was managing the New Vaudeville Band. He was approached by the manager of the post-Clapton Yardbirds, Simon Napier-Bell, to look after the group, as Napier-Bell was then moving into film productions:

"He came to see me, and one of the first things he said was, 'it's a good band but you need to find a guitarist. He's a real troublemaker that Jimmy Page.' I said, 'oh, why's that?' And he said, 'well, he's just a stirrer in the band.'

'So then I met the band and I said to Jimmy, 'I hear I have to give you the bullet 'cause you're a troublemaker.'

"'Troublemaker!' he said. 'You're dead right! We did *Blow Up*, four weeks in America and a Rolling Stones UK tour, and we got just 118 quid each.' I took them on."

It was late 1966. Grant forgot about the New Vaudeville Band.

His first act had been the Flinmtstones, a black band using brass who did backups

for visiting Americans, and for a while there had been a girlie group, the She Trinity ("A disaster" he says),.

But his career by then had already been checkered and colourful, prompted early on by the irony that his school in Battersea High St. was evacuated during the last war to Charterhouse.

"You can imagine!" he chortles. "The scum had arrived from Battersea. They loathed us. World War Two was on, and there was another war going on down there which nobody knew about.

"There used to be great battles, and we'd beat them up." Back in South-East London, his mother was working for the Church of England's Pension Board. His father he never actually knew.

After he left school he worked in a sheet metal factory the other side of Croydon, doing stage-hand jobs in the evenings at the Croydon Empire.

Then a bit in the catering business and a job as a photo sorter for Reuters before National Service, where he was stage manager for the monthly troop show in the local NAAFI hall.

After that it was the entertainment business for good, in one capacity or another.

Interspersed with the wrestling, film and TV work he was a general gig as a tour manager for the likes of Little Eva, Brian Hyland, Gene Vincent ("he was a bit of a loony - he drove cars at me"), Little Richard, Bee Bumble and the Stingers and Chuck Berry ("he could be a pain in the arse").

It was the same sort of lunacy, he says, as goes on now. The same silly things.

"I remember Tubby Hayes used to do all that farting and setting light to it.

"And when Vincent did some Sunday concerts with Emile Ford he used to always paint Ku Klux Klan signs on Emile's dressing room door.

"And generally there was always that groupie scene of those days; it was always there.

"From the Everlys to the opening act you were all on the bus. The coaches left from the side of the Planetarium; there used to be a London bus drivers' canteen there. You got a great closeness."

He was even there in Rome when Wee Willie Harris got banned from Italian TV - by the Pope, he thinks. Ah, Wee Willie. Until a few years ago he was still living with his parents in a prefab down the Old Kent Road.

By 1963, when the Great Group Explosion began to mushroom, he was an agent, working for Colin Berlin and Don Arden. He remembers going into a club and seeing the Alan Price Rhythm and Blues Combo.

He signed R&B groups the Animals and the Nashville Teens: "At that time I was making a deal to bring over Chuck Berry, and that was the blag to get the Animals to sign with the agency. They wanted to do the Chuck Berry tour and they wanted to record."

This gruel of experience, he believes, has been the recipe for his success as a manager - that, and instinct. He will slap the area of his heart and say that if something doesn't hit him there then he's obliged to stay away from it.

When he went to inspect the site at Knebworth, for the festival Zeppelin were originally due to play, he slapped his heart too, but on that occasion nothing happened.

All the same, this business now of lawyers and accountants in rock he considers pretty derisory, comparing it to the management of a rock band by a dental specialist, say.

"All I know," he says firmly, "is that if I 'adn't been a f - stagehand at the Croydon Empire for 15 bob a show, and if I 'adn't done all the things I have, like being a film extra and on the road with Gene Vincent and the rest, there's no way I could've coped with the events of the past five or six years."

These events, in toto, are notable for the way he's steered Zeppelin to the position of largest rock album sellers of all time.

Since the band went to Atlantic in 1968 Grant has made, it's estimated, 50 million dollars for the company. Their albums, right back to "Led Zeppelin One", still sell consistently. In the States they regularly do 60,000 units a month.

"Led Zeppelin Four" has been in the US charts for just under three years, "Houses Of The Holy" for 62 weeks.

The band's American tour last summer grossed four million dollars, probably the largest-ever by any rock act.

But Grant, like any true Englishman, doesn't care to talk about pay packets; not only is it vulgar, it's nobody's bloody business (the eager little brain and eyes of the taxman, my friend).

"I don't ask you about your earnings," he states bluntly, "so don't ask me about mine."

It's also out of order to suggest that he has created Zeppelin, Svengali-like, like some grand puppeteer; the band created themselves, as do all big bands, he believes.

He's simply established an environment - of the right deals and record companies - in which they can happen.

He thinks that if there's a strong, sympathetic relationship between the kids on the street and the artist, then the media can go take a flying eff.

He's long been suspicious of the media, and especially the BBC, whom he's attacked in the past for being too single-minded when Zeppelin, of course, have thought albums.

Specifically, he's still bitter about the lack of airplay for the band's first album, although the lack of response hardened his resolution to make it without singles and worked for the band, as well, in engendering a kind of underground mystique: the band that doesn't sell out and appear on television.

"Oh," he says now, picking at an old scab, "I s'pose the bottom line is, none of us is prepared to suck arse just to get bloody good music on state-controlled radio"

"We just decided not to put singles out because of that trip you have to go through, or had to at that time.

"It was always such an El Greaso Job! You had to go wine and dine all these people, and all that crap, and they weren't keen on anything that didn't sound poppy."

He rolls the word slowly around his mouth like it tasted kind of bad. "I think Led Zeppelin failed their audition."

Grant shrugs. "As long as the people wanna see you, you're all right, and that's the way it should be, shouldn't it? If musicians are talented and good, then why should they have to grease job the media?"

By the same token he thinks the BBC has exerted a wrong influence on the music scene.

"Or a misrepresentation of that scene. I mean, there's a lot of good bands that haven't made it because their records weren't played."

His protection of Zeppelin, in fact, is total, and not infrequently physical, too, which is generally the starting point for all those stories about Peter Grant the 'Eavy.

A couple of years back, at a time of the bootleg piracy, he was onstage in Vancouver, and looking down saw a man twiddling the dials of a large piece of apparatus with an aerial.

Since the man refused to identify himself, and Grant thought the officials weren't being sufficiently forceful, he picked it up himself and dropped it on the floor, whereupon there was no more apparatus.

But the guy, it turned out, was from the local Noise Abatement society and he swore out a warrant for Grant's arrest, though eventually it all got smoothed out with the mounties.

And then there was the infamous Jeffrey Collins incident.

Collins was a well-known London dealer in bootleg albums, and the story goes that Grant and some others went down to his shop and "disfigured" those pirate tapes which happened to be of Led Zeppelin.

"Mmm, I think we did confiscate them,"

Grant notes casually. "The funny thing was, he rang me up the next day and said Polydor (Zeppelin's distributing label in England then) had sent these people down and it was really disgusting how they'd treated him; he'd been terrified.

"He said one of the men was six feet three, weighed 18 and a half stone, had a beard, and was really vicious.

"It just shows you what the industry's coming to," I said.

"He didn't know who I was when I was in the shop. I told him: 'I think that's really disgusting of Polydor,' And he said, 'I knew you wouldn't approve of it.'

"Then the next day he rang back and said, 'Oh, all right, I know you've made a c - of me.' 'Well, we did 'ave a laugh.' I said, 'cause we recorded you on the phone.' We hadn't, but it was a parting shot."

Grant appeared on *24 Hours* after that episode, where he was asked about strongarm men and heavies in pop: "I said," he recalls, "whaddya mean 'heavies'? You ain't gonna get anybody heavier than me."

But he did appear to have gone further than most in campaigning against bootlegs.

"Well, they've got legislation together now, but before, all the record companies were doing was moaning to the press, never doing anything about it.

"Quite honestly, it was a con on the kids, because those albums were really crappy; they wore out quickly and were six quid each.

"It was a liberty, and when my information found out where the source was I decided to go and do something about it myself."

He's unrepentant of actions where his artists' well-being is concerned. "I think that's the right thing to do. When there were some people trying to videotape Bath Festival, and they'd already been told beforehand they couldn't, I have no qualms about throwing a bucket of water into the tape machine which blew the whole lot up."

He smiles broadly. "It was like a Will Hay thing. Whoosh! It made a horrible smell as it melted.

"But if somebody is doing something wrong, or being a s - to an artist that you manage...I mean, that's what they hire you for. I don't believe in pussyfooting around if it's my affair."

And the days of strongarm boys were over?

"I think all that got exaggerated, didn't it? But as far as I'm concerned as an archetypal heavy, most of those incidents have been on the spot situations, not sitting in Oxford St. and hiring a great crew of heavies to go round."

Mostly, however, he uses less controversial means to cosset Zeppelin. He ensures

they only make one album a year, to safeguard their physical and mental resources, and when he has the final tapes he hugs them jealously, delivering to the record company only what he chooses to deliver.

Recently he discovered that the components for the manufacture of classical records were put into a much cleaner acid bath than pop records, thus greatly reducing the risk of flaws, and promptly had that changed for the yearly immersion of Zeppelin material. If he had his way he wouldn't even give the record company the album cover until after the test pressing.

It's to do with the mentality of record companies, he explained. "As soon as they've got the record it isn't Led Zeppelin, Bad Company or Maggie Bell - it becomes matrix number so-and-so, and the marketing lads take over."

No doubt he has a healthy suspicion of anyone or anything that might cloud his Sussex idyll.

He says, for instance, that he's never ever rung Atlantic Records; it's a point of honour that they get in contact with him, "if they want the band."

Swansong, a small, independent company he's had in mind for two years, will give him even greater control of his own assets, though he's not greedy.

"We just want four or five acts that we could all add something to." The Pretty Things and possibly Roy Harper may be signed.

Not far from his mind is the memory from years ago of trying to do business in New York City with the huge GAC agency, when he himself was a still just a small-time agent in Britain.

Mincing for 20 minutes with the secretary while he waited to be shown in, the coffee out of a cardboard cup. That meant you weren't doing too well. But these days it's the plush Friar's club for lunch, because when you're hot you're hot.

"You go bleedin' cold, though," he says, a trifle sombrely, "and there's no way for you. If you're a manager and you don't have a hot act, you don't get in to see those people. They ain't even got the time of day for you."

But there's another memory, almost compensatory, of the days when he was a tour manager and he'd see these good, good artists turn up on Friday to collect their week's pay from managers who were as tough and insensitive as leather. He always felt bad about that.

"And I said to myself that if I ever became a manager I would never be like that. That's the main thing: doing the best you can. And staying by people, whatever happens." And he's bound to stick by it.

Graffiti on The Wall

The first half of 1975 was another heavy round of live work, with a further major US tour during the early spring, and a run of five hugely successful dates at London's Earls Court - Zeppelin's first UK gigs for over two years - in May. Sandwiched between came the new album, Physical Graffiti, a double LP which rounded up unused material from the previous projects, as well as more recent recordings. Again, this topped the charts in both the US and UK, and was far better received by critics than its immediate predecessor.

In the summer, with the group members winding down on individual holidays during a period of tax exile from the UK, Robert Plant and his wife were badly injured in a car crash on Rhodes. Plant was encased in plaster for some months, yet recovered sufficiently by November to allow the band to round off the year by completing work on a new album.

Plant: recording's no race for us

Chris Charlesworth in New York, February 1975

With two weeks of the current Led Zeppelin tour under his belt, Robert Plant is feeling the strain. One show has been cancelled because he caught the 'flu and he's still sniffing and talking like he's wearing a nose-clip.

Robert blames it partly on his particularly enjoyable Christmas festivities and the changes in climate involved in traversing the Atlantic.

We're talking in his suite at the Plaza Hotel in New York, the same suite just left by the Chairman of Sonesta Hotels, the chain that owns this particular chunk of Americana.

Love's "Forever Changes" album is playing on a tiny portable record player and Plant spreads out on a couch, bare-chested as always, golden hair curling everywhere and sipping a fruit drink (he needs his Vitamin C) between assaults on a paper handkerchief.

We begin by talking about the new album, "Physical Graffiti," due to be released any time. It's Zep's first double album.

"I suppose it was about a year ago when we started if I can cast my mind that far back," he says. "It's always a case of getting together and feeling out the moods of each of us when we meet with instruments for the first time in six months.

"We begin, as always, playing around and fooling about for two days, playing anything we want, like standards, our own material or anything that comes to us, and slowly but surely we

develop a feel that takes us on to the new material. Some of the new stuff came directly from this approach, like "Trampled Underfoot" which was just blowing out, and some comes from Jonesy or Pagey or myself - seldom myself - bringing along some structure which needs working on. Then the four of us inflict our own venom on it to develop the idea.

"We intended to record as much new stuff as we could before we started losing the fire, because we've always believed in not prolonging periods of recording or composition to such a degree where we know we are not up to our best. So we recorded as much fresh stuff as we could before looking back at some things we hadn't recorded. Then we saw that there was a lot of stuff we'd put down and we thought, 'why not put a double album out?' There's a lot of variation of material so it gives people a whole spectrum of style which is contained in one package and I think that's very good.

"It goes from one extreme to the other but at the same time it's very evident that it's Zeppelin. You could play a track on the radio that you'd think would never ever be us, but then when you listened you'd hear little things that couldn't be anyone else."

Robert agrees that 1974 was a year of little public activity for the group, but maintains that setting up their own label, Swan Song, took up much of their time.

"After the last American tour I was so relieved to be home again because I'd missed a season and I really need each season as it comes. I like to feel spring and I got back in August after that tour and realised I'd missed spring going into summer last year. I don't want to lose these perspectives in what I consider to be important for the lyrical content of what I write. I want to take stock of everything instead of going on the road until I don't know where the f — I am and end up like a poached egg three days old.

"But the time comes, as it does in recording and the record company and every move that we make, when we know it's time to go out on the road again. We all met and thought, 'what have we been doing?' "Obviously we had to rehearse the stuff from the new album to get it into some viable shape.

"We do 'Sick Again', which is about ourselves and what we see in Los Angeles, but it's a pity you can't hear the lyrics properly live. The lyrics say: 'From the window of a rented limousine, I saw your pretty blue eyes. One day soon, you're gonna reach sixteen, painted lady in the city of lies.' As much as it's pretty, it's sour really. That's exactly what LA stands for. Joni Mitchell summed it up best when she called it 'City of the Fallen Angels.'

"We do 'In My Time Of Dying' which is a really old, old standard thing. 'Gallows Pole' was an old traditional thing, too, and 'When The Levee Breaks' is something I have on an old album by Kansas Joe McCoy and Memphis Minnie in 1928. There are so many classics from way, way back to which we can give a little of ourselves to take them through the years."

It's now over two years since Zeppelin have appeared in Britain. Well Robert... "We shall definitely play England by hook or by crook before Midsummer Day this year. To say where and when at the moment is impossible as we haven't found out anything. All being well we shall definitely be in England soon during the summer.

"I play guitar now and again around Worcestershire but it isn't met by such tremendous outcries as it is when we all get together on stage.

I've been 75 per cent pleased with the shows we've done so far even though we've got a new stage set-up to get used to. It's quite hard to go out and confront thousands of people with a new stage, so we have to compensate for these new things.

"At the beginning of the tour I always feel nervous because I've got a lot to stand up for over here. If ever I've given all that I've got to give, it's been to an audience and the audiences here can really drain you until you're almost in tears.

"It's not as if these kids are all 17 or 18 and going barmy. These people have been going along with us for seven or eight years. Now I know there's people in England who'll say they've been standing with us for seven or eight years, but over here the whole motion is like a seven-year trek that's charged with the energy that these people give. My nerves are really through, hoping that I can re-establish the contact that I had before.

"The English promotion side of things has always been archaic. They didn't want to know us as the New Yardbirds in the early days, so we had to come over here and make a statement that no-one else had made before. Then everybody wanted to know.

"I can see this happening again with the Pretty Things who have achieved so much ability with their writing and playing. They get much more coverage here than in England, but how much coverage can you get in England, anyway? It's not too hot, and the promoters are a little reserved in what they can promote."

Zeppelin have always maintained a reputation as outlaws of the road in the US. Talk of their excesses in hotel rooms ranges far and wide, and the faint of heart have been known to cower when they approach with the twinkle in their eyes that spells havoc.

"Like the music, the legend grows too," said Robert. "There are times when people need outlets. We don't rehearse them and, let's face it, everybody's the same. Over the last few years we've spent some of our time at the Edgewater Inn in Seattle where Bonzo fishes for sharks in the sea from his bedroom window. Hence the mudshark thing on the Zappa album.

"No, we're not calming down yet. Calming down doesn't exist until you're dead. You just do

whatever you want to do when you want to do it, provided there's no nastiness involved, then the karma isn't so good."

Moving on to more serious topics, I asked whether Robert thought "Stairway to Heaven" was becoming heavily identified as the group's signature tune. "I don't know about that. We've always intended to try and create a spectrum of music that captures as many aspects of us as we could, although we never realised it at the begin-

ning. We try and do this on stage, too. We start off like songs of thunder and then we take it down with a song like 'Rain Song', so you tend to develop a rapport rather than just a blatant musical statement. It ebbs and flows through two and a half hours or so, and we feel it would be unfair for the climax to be 'Whole Lotta Love' now, because that isn't where we climax any more.

"It's quite a moving thing. I remember doing it at the Garden last year and I sang well away from

Left

Flamboyant clothes for a flamboyant stageshow

Right

John Bonham at 'multi-miked' see-through perspex drum kit

the mike and I could hear 20,000 people singing it. I mean…20,000 people singing 'High Heeled Sneakers' is one thing, but 20,000 people singing 'Stairway to Heaven' is another. People leave satisfied after that, and I don't think they leave satisfied because of the violent aspects of the music, which I don't think exist anyway, but because they feel a satisfaction with the music they've heard."

The ultimate trip

Michael Oldfield, May 24, 1975

It's not very often that the opportunity of experiencing the very best of something presents itself; when it does come along, it's inevitably only appreciated in retrospect. Yet before Led Zeppelin had got far into their set at London's Earls Court on Sunday, it became obvious this was the definitive rock performance; so much so that it's inconceivable that another band could do as well.

In the space of nearly three-and-a-half hours, they covered virtually every variation of rock and left no doubt they could triumph with any style they had omitted.

They can do this because Zeppelin stand at the very heart of rock: the blues/rock 'n' roll-based style typified by "Whole Lotta Love," supported by a firm grounding in the English rock tradition, evident on their acoustic numbers.

This is the base for development and, as they improvise around these themes, they draw utilise elements of jazz and classical music to build up a complete picture of contemporary rock.

For fleeting seconds it's possible to hear traces of every major British band around - not just more obvious examples like Deep Purple or Black Sabbath, but even Yes and Emerson, Lake and Palmer.

Naturally, they never fully explore these various avenues; should they ever do so it would be interesting to see how they compare. On the evidence to be gleaned on Sunday night, they'd probably perform them better.

But the most immediately impressive feature of Led Zeppelin live is not so much the superb music as the assurance with which they produce it. There's nothing apologetic about them, no "little numbers from our latest album."

They're so big and so good there's no need to plug albums or make excuses for songs written long ago - and they know it. Some might interpret this as arrogance; in fact, it's just part of the band's no-nonsense approach. They go on stage to play music, not to boost either their own or the audience's egos.

This authority, though, manifests itself in an absolute power which few other bands can even hope for, and that could sway an audience any way the band wishes.

Wisely, they don't choose to use it that way; there's no need to whip up the fans or repeatedly ask if everyone feels all right. Packing 17,000 people into Earls Court on five separate occasions - never mind those who couldn't get tickets - is all the proof they need of their power.

Their self-assurance is no more evident than in their stage act. With video cameras beaming close-ups of every movement on to a screen high above their heads, Plant and Page pose and strut, proud as peacocks, lords of the jungle.

Plant thrusts his navel into a camera lens and

if the music wasn't absolutely first class. With sound problems and endless tune-ups utterly non-existent, they played brilliantly and with practised ease that made the music flow in such a fast stream it was impossible to absorb it all in one sitting.

Page and Jones don't have to face each other and trade licks; they both know what they've got to do and they KNOW that they will do it right.

Led Zeppelin look very much like four individuals when they are on stage. It's in the music itself that they meet and fit together perfectly.

So what of the

disdainfully shakes the hair out of his eyes; Page makes his gravity-defying backward bends and describes an 180 degree arc with his arm between a series of ear-splitting chords.

John Paul Jones and John Bonham take no part in this performance. Jones hugs the shadows, and when the cameras catch him, he's wearing a look of quiet intensity; while Bonham is mostly grim-faced as he piles on the pressure - the stoker of the Zeppelin express.

None of this would be worth much, of course,

music? As Plant gleefully pointed out, the media had got it wrong (again) and this wasn't Zeppelin's American show.

After three shortish numbers - opening with a rousing "Rock And Roll" - they began a journey through the soul of the band.

It had little to do with chronology; both old and new were presented side by side, recording the highlights of their six-and-a-half year "relationship." It reached an incredible high with their reworking of the blues on "In My Time Of Dying"

Opposite

Plant and Page. The mellower side of a wild show. The acoustic set returns for the Earl's Court performances

Left

Plant struts Stateside, USA 1975

Below

Jones with electric mandolin during 'Going To California'

- and just kept climbing higher and higher.

Jones switched on to keyboards for "The Song Remains The Same," Page proving with a beautifully laid-back solo that he's not just the one-high-energy-solo man he's sometimes accused of being, and stayed there for "Kashmir," surely Led Zep's finest (recorded) hour.

It's an atypical Zeppelin song, highly structured, with little room for extended improvisation. Page, incredibly, found the space and made full use of it. Bonham pounded out the beat, Plant soared, his voice spitting out lines like "this WASTED land," and his end of song credit - "John Paul Jones: a rather cheap orchestra" - summed up Jones' swirling chords that give the song its atmosphere.

Yet John Paul had just started. He moved in "No Quarter," taking it through the changes from rock to almost classical and then picking out a funky riff - the cue for Page to come in with a solo that, judging by the smile that crept across his face as the number reached its climax, pleased him greatly.

Then, a new departure: four-part harmonies for "Tangerine." No trouble.

In keeping with the gentle mood of that song, out came the farmhouse chairs and acoustic guitars for a peaceful three-song break, Jones, Plant and Page just sitting and playing simply.

They roared back with a stomping, driving "Trampled Underfoot": the very essence of pure rock. And then - a surprise dedication for MM's Chris Welch: "This is the one you've been waiting for, Chris. Remember that snare drum?" What else could it be but Bonham's solo, "Moby Dick?" Under such circumstances, it seems inappropriate for me to comment, other than to report that it included some remarkable quad effects.

Page's turn next for the super-sound treatment. A completely restructured "Dazed and Confused," sounding even fresher than the original, brought out the violin bow.

Only one song could follow: an imaculate "Stairway To Heaven" which rounded off three hours (to the dot) of superb music.

Bonham: over the hills and far away

Chris Welch goes down on the farm...to meet Led Zep's drummer June 21, 1975

Gossip in the village was running riot. John up at the farm was going to buy The Chequers. The American in the bar of another public house a few miles distant was adamant. So was the landlord, and a few grizzled farmers, as they downed pints of the finest beer known to men of science and agriculture.

But the object of the debate emitted a stentorian bellow that scotched the rumours once and for all. "No I'm not buying the bloody Chequers! Mind you I was interested."

John Bonham, farmer, stockbreeder, and drummer with the world's heaviest rock band, was supping in a Worcestershire haven of low beams and convivial company.

The day before, his wife Pat had given birth to a baby daughter, Zoe, and there was plenty of cause for celebration. And apart from a small matter of being banned from driving for six months (no rumours here - it was all in the local paper), John was feeling that contentment and satisfaction most enjoyed by a self-made man.

A few weeks before he had been pounding his massive drum kit in another world again. The world of thousands of admiring rock fans, enormous record sales and marathon, sell-out concerts. He seems equally at home in both, and he applies the same direct, furious energy.

At the historic Earls Court concerts, Bonham's bombastic, metronomic drumming was an essential factor in a band that needs a regular supply of adrenalin. Bonham summons his reserves of

strength from a tough, well-built body that was honed in the building industry as much as the music, industry.

John pours out his ideas, opinions and thoughts in a tone that brooks no argument, and yet he has a fearless warmth and humour that command respect. He looks the world straight in the eye, and expects the same treatment. No shrinking violet then, this man who was once told there was no call for his kind of loud, aggressive drumming.

And yet it's hardly a coincidence that when the men of rock, who deal in volume, flash and fame, reap the rich rewards of their craft, they head for the hills and vales, far from the stink of the city, there to enjoy the animals, earth and silence.

Bonham's spread is a bit like the Ponderosa in Bonanza. After driving on stilted motorways through the smog of Birmingham (a living memorial to Sixties "planning"), the country's scars gradually heal, and the Worcestershire countryside blossoms.

A ranch-style nameboard appears around a bend in a B-road, and twin white fences accom-

Left

Page takes a bow.

Earls Court, May 1975

Top

Jones and Plant.

A light-hearted moment,

Earls Court

Bottom

'All that glitters is gold'

pany a long, straight driveway to the modern brick farmhouse, where the gaffer and his family are ensconced.

Had John always intended to go into farming? "Never, I was never into farming at all, I wasn't even looking for a farm, just a house with some land. But when I saw this place, something clicked, and I bought it back in '72."

John seems to have been cheerfully accepted into the farming community, and is anyway guaranteed of at least one friendly neighbour.

Robert Plant lives just a few miles away surrounded by goats which John avows "eat everything, old boots, you name it."

John gave a great guffaw that could probably be heard halfway round the hundred acres of sheep and cattle that surround the house.

We set off for a stump round the fields. The view was breathtaking, apart from an unfortunate line of recently constructed electricity pylons.

One of the old barns has been converted to the special needs of the modern rock and roll farmer.

"This is the hot car shop," said John with a chuckle, leading the way past the coven of cats who had been following us at a discreet distance. And there, squashed together in the darkness, stood a trio of highly improbable vehicles.

An elaborately painted contraption that resembled a pre-war taxicab, mounted

Left

'Avening Angels'. Tne Awesome Foursome live at Earls Court, London. These were epic concerts with simultaneous video screen projections. There was a massive demand for tickets with fans queueing over 24 hours in advance of sale

Right

Page displaying his dragon suit

Far right

'From session men to superstars',

The Triumphant Homecoming

on wheels a yard wide, was, John explained: "a show car. I bought her in Los Angeles. She can do 150 mph. And that one is a '67 Chevette with a seven-litre engine.

"This one is a 1954 two-door Ford with an eight-litre engine. You get guys going past in a

John once bought himself a Rolls Royce.

"It was a white one. I went to a wedding reception in Birmingham. When I came out it looked like a bomb had hit it. All these skinheads had jumped on it. They kicked in the windscreen, smashed everything. If it had been any other sort of car they would have left it alone."

Red rags to the bull obviously. But John has worked and still works hard for his

sports car who think it's an old banger, until I put my foot down.

"It's an amazing car, look at all the chrome inside. She'd only done 10,000 when I bought her."

Like many enjoying success for the first time,

seven-litre crust.

Back in the house we talked about his early days and the drumming career that has earned him world renown.

"This used to be just a three-bedroomed house. My father did all the wood panelling, and I did a lot of the work with my brother and sub-contractors.

"If you have builders in they'll make excuse after excuse about delays during the

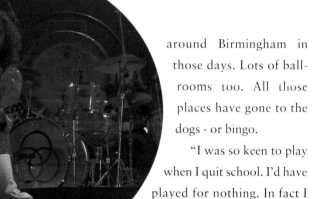

summer so that they can have work inside during the bad weather.

"I know, because when I left school I went into the trade with my dad. He had a building business and I used to like it.

"But drumming was the only thing I was any good at, and I stuck at that for three or four years. If things got bad I could always go back to building.

"I had a group with Nicky James, an incredible lead singer. But we had so much of the equipment on hire purchase, we'd get stopped at night on the way back from a gig and they'd take back all the PA.

"Nicky had a big following then, and he could sing in any style. But he just couldn't write his own material.

"We used to have so many clubs we could play around Birmingham in those days. Lots of ballrooms too. All those places have gone to the dogs - or bingo.

"I was so keen to play when I quit school. I'd have played for nothing. In fact I did for a long time. But my parents stuck by me.

"No, I never had any drum lessons. But I remember Carl (Carl Palmer) went, he had a lot of lessons. I just played the way I wanted, and got black-listed in Birmingham. 'You're too loud!' they used to say. 'There's no future in it.'

"But nowadays you can't play loud enough. I just wish there was a way of wiring a drum kit to get the natural sound through the PA. I've tried so many different ways, but when you're playing with a band like ours you get so many problems with sound.

"With Jimmy and John Paul on either side playing lead, they can leak into the drum mikes, and if you have too many monitors you start to get feedback. I never get it the way I want."

And yet Bonham's drum sound was fairly fantastic at Earls Court, I thought.

"I enjoyed those concerts," says John. "I thought they were the best shows that we've ever put on in England. I always get tense before a show, and we were expecting trouble with such a huge audience.

"But everything went really well and, although we couldn't have the laser beams at full power, I thought the video screen was well worth doing. It

cost a lot of bread, but you could see close-ups you'd never be able to see normally at a concert. It was worth every penny."

Did the band rehearse for weeks on end before their concerts?

"Nah, three days. Mind you, it was only a few weeks before we got back from the States. We just needed a bit of rust remover.

"We had already done a lot of planning for that States tour, because we like to change the show each year. There's nothing worse than playing the old numbers over and over again.

"You've got to keep in some of the old songs of course. I don't know what would happen if we didn't play 'Stairway to Heaven,' because it's become one of the biggest things we've ever done.

"When Jimmy plays the first chord in the States, it's like instant bedlam, until Robert comes in with the first line.

"And we always play 'Whole Lotta Love' because people want to hear it, and I still get a great kick out of 'Dazed and Confused.'

"I always enjoy the number because we never play it the same. With the other stuff, we'll put one in, or take one out.

"On the last night at Earls Court we played 'Heartbreaker,' 'Black Dog,' and a bit from 'Out On The Tiles.' With the songs from 'Physical Graffiti' we've got such a wide range of material.

"It wasn't done on purpose. It's just that we went through a stage where we were very conscious of everything we played. We felt it had to be a certain kind of thing for Zeppelin.

"Now we record everything that comes up and, of course, in the States they play it on the radio so the people know what we're doing.

Right

'The Power and The Glory'.

Amidst the Glam and Glitter era,

Zeppelin represented true

musicianship. The shows at Earls

Court ran for over three hours,

using a 300,000 watt PA system

providing crystal clear sound

"In Britain we never get any airplay except from John Peel and Alan Freeman. In the States they'll play 'Trampled Underfoot' all day.

"When we first ran through it, John Paul and Jimmy started off the riff, but then we thought it was a bit souly for us. Then we changed it around a bit. It's great for me. Great rhythm for a drummer. It's just at the right pace and you can do a lot of frills.

"But compare that to 'Dazed and Confused.' The speed of the thing! While we're playing, I think 'Christ if I drop one, knit one and purl one - that's it.' You've gotta be fit to play that one, and if I don't feel too good, it's very hard.

"We keep tapes of every show, and it's very useful afterwards, especially for my drum solo, because then I can hear what works best."

Despite John's burly appearance and confident mien, it's a fact that he suffers from doubt and worry just before every Zeppelin concert. He'll sit backstage, nervously tapping sticks, anxious to get on stage and stuck into their exhausting three hour show.

"I've actually got worse - terrible bad nerves all the time.

"Once we start into 'Rock And Roll' I'm fine. I just can't stand sitting around, and I worry about playing badly, and if I do, then I'm really p——off. If I play well, I feel great.

"Everybody in the band is the same, and each has some little thing they do before we go on, just like pacing about, or lighting a cigarette. It used to be even worse at festivals.

"You might have to sit around for a whole day, and of course you daren't drink, because you'll get tired out and blow it. So you sit drinking tea in a caravan, with everybody saying 'far out man.'

"We don't do festivals so much now because of the amount of equipment we have. There's all the PA and lights and the black floor for the stage. Imagine the changeover between us and the Floyd! It would take hours! The Bath festivals were the only ones we ever played here, and they went really well."

Left

Page plays acoustic

Below

'And it makes me wonder!'

One of the features of Bonham's marathon drum solos during the Earls Court concerts was the special effects employed on the tympani. Had he been using a synthesiser?

"No, it was just phasing on the pedal tymps. I was using them in '73. It's just a different sound.

"Not everybody likes or understands a drum solo, so I like to bring in effects and sounds to keep their interest. I've been doing the hand drum solo for a long time - before I joined Zeppelin.

"I remember playing a solo on 'Caravan' when I was 16. Sometimes you can take a chunk out of your knuckles on the hi-hat or you can catch your

hand on the tension rods.

"I try to play something different every night on the solo, but the basic plan is the same, from sticks to hands and then the tymps, and the final build up.

"It would be really boring to play on the straight kit all the time. On the last States tour I was really chuffed when I had some good reviews from people who don't even like drum solos.

"I usually play for twenty minutes, and the longest I've ever done was under thirty. It's a long time, but when I'm playing it seems to fly by.

"Sometimes you come up against a blank and you think 'how am I going to get out of this one?' Or sometimes you go into a fill and you know halfway through it's going to be disastrous.

"There have been times when I've blundered, and got the dreaded look from the lads. But that's a good sign. It shows you're attempting something you've not tried before."

Was there any danger of John losing power in time in view of his arduous years on the road? "I'm not losing strength. I'm less tired after a solo than I used to get in the early days. Of course we didn't have a break for the acoustic numbers then.

"But it was so cold at Earls Court, we had to have an electric fire in the dressing room. The unions wouldn't let us use blow heaters. I had a run through on the Friday night before the first show, and I was playing in an overcoat."

One of the mysteries of Zeppelin is that they have never put themselves out for a hit single, and "Graffiti" had obvious singles chart potential. Didn't they want one?

"No, not really. It's because of the length of a piece like 'Trampled Underfoot.' It's not worth cutting something out just for the sake of a single. And if people like Led Zeppelin they would have bought the LP anyway. No - it would be pointless

to put a single out from the album."

After a sojourn at the pub, we returned to the farmhouse to sample some brandy and the delights of a quad sound system that threatened to stampede the sleeping herds of Herefords.

"Listen to this, it's great.." John put on the Pretty Things' new single "I'm Keeping." They're a band who seem to be enjoying a whole new lease of life since they signed to Swansong, Zeppelin's own label. He was also raving about Supertramp's album and admitted a new interest in country and western music.

"I wish there were some more live bands around here I could have a blow with," sighed John, tossing back a brandy, and barely audible above the thunder of speakers.

"There's nowhere for them to play - now it's all discos. God, I hate those places. It's all right if you're out for a night on the tiles. But I like to hear a good live group. You've gotta remember - they're the backbone of the business."

But in case the rock business starts to dry up, John is setting his nine-year-old son Jason on the right path. He has a junior drum kit in front of dad's juke box and pounds away to Gary Glitter.

But John is not sure if he'll take the right path to becoming another drummer rock superstar. He came home from the Cubs during the afternoon clutching his latest single, "Whispering Grass" by Windsor Davies.

"You can't teach him anything," warned John. "He's got a terrible temper."

Left and Right

'Curtain Call' 85,000 fans

witnessed Zeppelin over 5

magical nights at London's

Earls Court, May 1975.

These were to be the

band's final indoor

appearances

Song Remains the Same

In a year without any touring or live work, Led Zeppelin's audience instead had the unprecedented treat of two album releases. The first, in April, was Presence, the set completed the previous December. In now familiar fashion, this album was housed in an enigmatic sleeve, minus band or title credit (a design which again had caused a release delay). It tended to polarise critical opinion (particularly in the UK where the punk reaction was starting to stir), but again had no trouble pleasing the fans, and topped the charts on both sides of the Atlantic. Seven months later, it was followed by the double album soundtrack, recorded live three years earlier at Madison Square Garden, of the finally released film The Song Remains The Same. This topped the UK chart, and made No.2 in America, as the movie itself did excellent business in both countries - again despite sniping from certain critics and reviewers.

Led Zeppelin Chapter 94

by Roy Carr, February 26th 1976

In terms of widespread public confidence, it appears that the law of diminishing returns doesn't apply to Led Zeppelin.

Nine years and almost as many albums since their maiden flight, NME's Readers' Poll indicates that in these times of uncertainty, Led Zeppelin's stock is as stable as Gilt-Edged Securities.

Whilst other bands of Zeppelin's stature fall apart at the seams, lose their incentive, grow complacent, or become riddled with paranoia, Zeppelin give the impression of being utterly immune from such occupational hazards.

Every major band must dread the inevitable day when they awake to find that the public that once fawned over them has deserted them in favour of a fresh face. Whilst not exactly fresh-faced, the emergence of rock's fourth generation - a movement that has brought about suspicion, insecurity and the first major generation gap inside the little world of rock'n'roll since the 50s - has caused more panic amongst the league leaders than any Poll result.

Waves have been made.

In the first punk fusillade aimed at the rock establishment, almost no one was spared. However, whilst most of rock's patriarchs were rightly stigmatized as Old Farts, Jimmy Page and Robert Plant seemed to hold a strange fascination for The Angry Young Men of the New Wave.

The fact that Page and Plant could casually wander into the lion's den, check out what (given time) could eventually become strong competition, and then voice their approval, gained Zeppelin the respect that the rest of rock's pampered aristocracy failed to receive from a justifiably restless proletariat.

If anything, Robert Plant has assumed the role of sympathetic big kid brother to many young bands. This afternoon, as Zeppelin go about putting the final touches to their new road show at Manti-

core's desolate rehearsal studio in Fulham, members of Generation X scurry around the stage in the ill-fitting raincoats, firing smart-ass one-liners at Plant and receiving just as good as they give.

"C'mon lads", Plant chortles as he fends off a good-natured jibe. "I know it's still a bit early in the day, but you've got to learn to be much quicker than that."

Swaggering around the stage in a velvet-trimmed, gold lamé drape jacket, Plant proudly demonstrates Zeppelin's latest toy - an electronic harmoniser.

"Wellah Hulloo, Ahh-Mahrey Loo, Ahh-Good-er Bah Hhheart", he burbles plum-in-cheek into a microphone and through the wonders of modern technology, promptly gets the sound of two synchronised voices in perfect harmony for the price of one.

"'Ere...you have a go", Plant says as he hands over the microphone to bleached Billy Idol. "This thing can make you sound like The Everly Brothers".

Idol grabs hold of the microphone, grins at his mates, shakes a shoulder at Plant and starts bellowing "A Whole Lotta Love". The Lemon Squeezer smiles approvingly.

Originally the assignment was this: get the individual members of Zeppelin to select and discuss three tracks apiece for a hypothetical "Best Of Led Zeppelin" compilation.

John Paul Jones picks up the entire stash of Zeppelin albums, flicks through the sleeves as though he's never seen them before and politely enquires: "Can we listen to them all first?"

The idea is promptly jettisoned.

To say that Zeppelin are more than a little chuffed by their landslide victory in the NME Poll would be an understatement.

"It only goes to prove", insists Page, "that Led Zeppelin are not a nostalgia band."

Everyone in the room nods in agreement.

"The very essence", adds Plant, "of why you're talking to Zeppelin as four people all in the same room is because we still excite each other. It's not a stagnant situation whereby we're just going through the paces."

Usually, the longer bands stay together, the less reason they find for continuing. Not only do they find it increasingly difficult to produce new material, but the actual physical effort of getting out of bed and gathering together in the same studio on the same

Left

Page and Jones discuss

musical arrangements

Right

Page and Plant relax

talking to the Music Press

day becomes a mammoth operation in itself.

Led Zeppelin, it appears, aren't bothered by such problems.

The atmosphere that prevails at a Led Zeppelin rehearsal is hardly melodramatic. Nobody plays prima donna and neither is it a calculated exercise in putting together a crowd-baiting three ring circus.

In the bleak atmosphere of a disembowelled cinema, Zeppelin run down "The Song Remains

The Same" with as much enthusiasm as if performing before a crowd of 10,000 - and not just a dozen roadies and two large industrial heaters.

"I think", says Page, "that if you've got a set that's so cut and dried, so well-rehearsed that you've no other option but to play it note-for-note each night, then it's bound to get stagnant.

"We've always structured things so that there's an element in which we can suddenly shoot off on something entirely different and see what's hap-

pening. Personally speaking, for me, that's where the element of change and surprise comes in – the possibilities of having that kind of freedom, should you suddenly require it, right in the middle of a number.

"You never quite know what's waiting around the corner. The last time, it was 'Presence'. For that album we all agreed that we'd go right back to square one. Start with nothing, just a few basic structures and the minimum of rehearsal. We completed the album in less than two weeks.

'We have fulfilled our destiny. We stood against everything – chance, the elements, existence itself. The doors of creation are always open. (Don't go away. There's more) It now goes beyond how much one grosses on the gate. The bread doesn't matter anymore, we still care enough to go plonking around the world yet again'

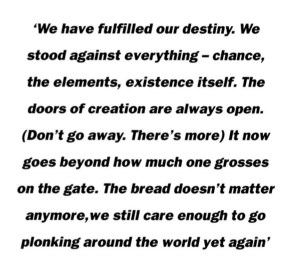

"That's why", Page elaborates, "'Presence' was a testament...if you like, two fingers" (he gestures) "to all the kinds of things that destroy other bands. We needed to do that album in so much as we had been together a long time and that we required the challenge of working fast and simple."

Plant maintains that, though every album has been important in Led Zeppelin's development, "Presence" was the most crucial. With Bonham and

Jones signalling their endorsement, Plant reveals that if there has ever been the remotest chance of Zeppelin calling it quits, that was the juncture.

"We've never never reached a stage when we've turned to each other in despair and said where do we go from here? But when we recorded 'Presence' we were fighting to survive."

It was a test of endurance which they only just managed to pass.

"I feel", Plant begins slowly, "that in some ways we have fulfilled our Destiny." He pauses. "But by the same reckoning, there's absolutely no end to the fulfilment. The doors of creation are always open.

"'Presence' was our stand against everything. Our stand against The Elements, against Chance. We were literally fighting against Existence itself. We'd left home for 12 months and it seemed that everything was about to crumble."

Plant, his body severely shattered as a result of an auto wreck, his wife Maureen similarly in a critical condition, was just one of the dilemmas confronting Zeppelin and The Future. After careful consideration of the situation, it was agreed that the best therapeutic treatment for Plant was to become absorbed in recording a new album.

Still in extreme pain, he was nightly wheeled from his hotel, through sub-zero conditions and into Munich's Musicland Studios.

"We all knew that maybe it wouldn't come together - but there's absolutely no doubt about it, that album helped pull me through at a time when I just couldn't have taken any more. There's no getting away from the fact that we had our backs up against the wall, but we were determined that

Below

Page, on Gibson SG

guitar, jams with

Ron Wood of The Rolling

Stones at Charity concert

in Plumpton

Right

A Tribute to Johnny Kidd

and The Pirates

nothing was going to stop us. Once we got into the studio, it just happened spontaneously.

"If ever there was a time to quit that was it, because before we went to Musicland, we didn't actually know if we'd ever play together again or, if we did stop, just how long we'd have to wait - and whether or not it would ever be the same should we get back together again.

"That's why, alone of all the albums we've recorded, 'Presence' relates specifically to a point in time. 'Presence' isn't a precis on aspects of Life In General, but aspects of hurt. That's what songs like 'Tea For One' and 'Hots On For Nowhere' are all about."

He emphasises the point by reciting the second verse of "Hots On For Nowhere":

"Now I've got friends who will give me their shoulder In event I should happen to fall And time and his bride growing older I got friends who will

give me fuck all."

"I was Questioning Everything," he explains. Bands have thrown in the towel for less. Plant continues to speak for the rest of Zeppelin when he concedes that most bands bring about their own downfall, be it either through apathy or plain stupidity. One gets tired, almost cynical, of musicians quitting bands over "irrevocable differences of musical policy" and a burning desire to cut a solo album. In nine years, there's never been any serious suggestions of anyone taking an extended sabbatical from Zeppelin in order to record a solo Meisterwerk.

"Well", enquires Plant, "who are we gonna make solo albums with? There's nobody better than this band to play with and nobody better to help you. Sure, one's imagination is a great thing but it isn't nearly as good as bouncing ideas off one another! You can really only achieve a personal peak after being around certain people for any length of time."

But you know the drill. I've written a dozen songs but nobody in the band wants to record any of them!

Page chimes in: "It's all down to the question of the importance of being happy and content within the framework of the group you're a member of. Sufficiently happy enough not to feel the need to go off and make a solo album. Now for quite some time The Beatles had that kind of mutual contentment.

"I was in New York, and I can remember McCartney telling me at the time he was cutting his second solo album that it was difficult for him to play with other musicians.

"McCartney felt that, on his own, it was an uphill struggle. He didn't know the musicians and apart from his reputation as a Beatle, they didn't know him. He didn't realise the immense difficulties until he was suddenly confronted with that specific problem."

McCartney isn't the only one who has found out the hard way. After innumerable solo albums, it is rumoured that The Who have discussed the prospects of using one another as sessioners on individual projects.

"Well", says Page, "it's taken them long enough to reach that conclusion - but isn't that because, in terms of virtually everything The Who undertake, Townshend plays Fuehrer?"

Though Zeppelin insist that "Presence" was their major recent endeavour, NME readers nominated the soundtrack "The Song Remains The Same" as their premier choice for '76. It's safe to assume that much of Led Zeppelin's runaway victory has been achieved through the film and its soundtrack. Despite the fact that in some quarters (notably in this publication), "The Song Remains TheSame"was received with "certain reservations", it seems to be the perfect fulfilment of the average Zeppelinite's heavy metal fantasy.

Originally premiered in four-track stereo, "The Song Remains The Same" is currently being shown with mixed-down two-track, since outside the capital, very few cinemas are equipped with the requisite facilities.

Indeed, in some locations the house management have been less than co-operative. This has meant that Jimmy Page and Robert Plant have been moving around Great Britain making spot

sound-checks at showcase engagements.

Both agree that in Birmingham the management of the cinema was most sympathetic towards their distinguished guests, despite the fact that on the opening night, the house equipment blew in the last few frames.

"Apart from that", Page admits, "it really has proved to be a hard battle against the cinema circuits and their managers. Obviously, one tries to be idealistic about such things, but it's not possible to do what you want on the regular cinema circuits in the United Kingdom."

"I wouldn't be risking the use of my leg and going out on such a lengthy tour it I felt that it really wasn't worth it. If I and the rest of the band didn't honestly feel that there was something to achieve we'd stay at home.

"You have to understand, it now goes far beyond how much one can gross on the gate. The bread doesn't come into it any more. Never mind the prissy things - that's something 'Presence' taught us.

"No matter what some people may think, we still care enough to go plonking off around the world yet again."

Darkening Skies

A year of mixed triumph and tragedy. In April, following a few weeks' delay due to Robert Plant being ill, Zeppelin began their biggest US tour yet, due to run in three separate stages until August. They played to some of their largest-ever audiences (70,000-plus), though two dates were cut short, one through Page falling ill, and the other through heavy rain making their stage equipment dangerous. A highlight during one of the breaks saw them back in England to collect an Ivor Novello award for Sevices To British Music, but a July concert in California was marred by Peter Grant and others being arrested for beating up a backstage security man. Then, at a New Orleans date, Robert Plant got the horrifying news

from home that his five-year-old son Karac had died of a stomach infection. The rest of the tour was cancelled, the grieving Plant went into seclusion, and many considered the group to have effectively ended.

Plant: new wave is good - I just wish the music was more original

Robert Plant talks to Ray Coleman, June 25th 1977

The Robert Plant lounging in his hotel suite, playing blues albums by Elmore James, is a far cry from the preening, swaggering stage figure who, half an hour previously, had been the focal point for 20,000 pairs of eyes at Madison Square Garden, New York.

Now, with a beer in his hand and his feet bare, he's what the Americans would call "a regular guy" - normal, almost formal, relaxed, reflective.

Led Zeppelin's public face, 28-year-old Plant has a wry sense of humour, and tonight, in the midst of the band's six-night stint in New York, he's eager to talk about their past, present and future; his very real fears that his foot injury might have spelled doom to his career as a singer; the state of the punk rock industry; his role as a vocalist and relationship with the rest of the band; what we can expect from Zeppelin in the years ahead.

Two years have elapsed since much has been

heard of Zeppelin. There was the stultifying boredom of the film The Song Remains The Same, but apart from this - silence.

Now, they reappear on a long American tour

in top gear, and even Plant is forced to comment on the fact that he's smiling almost permanently at the tjoys of being back in harness and finding his foot, injured in a car accident in Greece, to benot too much of a handicap on stage.

Despite the lay-off, he says, he had experienced little initial stage-fright because they went through a rigorous two-month rehearsal. They had to. With no new album from which to draw, they had to first get used to playing together and then work out new applications of material from "Physical Graffiti" and older records.

"So I was really at home with the idea of playing. The only thing I didn't know about was whether I was going to be able to pace myself out, with my foot problems. For the first two or three gigs I was really measuring every move I made, to find if I'd gone too far or whatever.

"The first gig in Dallas, Texas, I was petrified. Since Earls Court in London, all this horrendous physical hoo-ha had taken place and for the ten minutes before I walked up those steps in Dallas I was cold with fright.

"Supposing I couldn't move around the stage properly, because my right foot is permanently enlarged now? Well, it was killing for the first two gigs. I had to be virtually carried back on one foot.

"But once I'd got it used to the concussive knocks of stage work, it was OK and now I've paced myself so I can work without anyone, hopefully, realising that I have this thing to live with.

"The thing is, I don't really know what I'm doing with my body when I'm playing and I just throw myself around the stage instinctively. But Dallas was the worry: I thought about what would happen if the foot wouldn't take it.

"Yet when I walked up the steps to the stage, all the premonitions and anxieties washed away, and the exhilaration took over I thought: 'Ah, it's been SO LONG' and I just loved being back up there - and I was a looney again!"

And the crowds had been great. To work live was, in Zeppelin's plan for The Big Return, a stimulus for any new albums they intended after such a spell of inactivity. But they had difficulties with the programme.

No new album meant they were "trading on past glories," as Plant described it. And using material people were familiar with, they had the challenge of giving people something above and beyond what they had already seen, because who wanted a Zeppelin stage re-run of two or three years ago?

This was achieved by bringing back the acoustic set for the first time in America for about seven years, and introducing songs like "Battle Of Evermore" - previously rejected because Sandy Denny featured on the record, and so they couldn't accurately re-create it on stage - and taking the odd risk.

"To begin with, people were a little bit restless. They didn't know what the hell was going on. Kept looking at us, presumably thinking: Are they really THAT old? But because of the way in which we've taken the challenge of re-working some of our old material and introducing some unlikely aspects of it into stage work, that way we've gone a stage farther again."

For the first few concerts, they would look sheepishly at each other on stage. No one spoke, but the question each seemed to be asking was: are we getting it right?

"Suddenly it burst through after six gigs, so that by the time we got to places like St. Louis, it had taken on another level of control, rather than merely trotting out the old favourites - for example, John Paul Jones is getting far more involved now, he's the sort of man-of-the-match!"

And so, says Plant, he seemed to be finding himself smiling all the time now - "like some grinning goon at the Talk of the Town" - because they had triumphed with the programme, and most of all because he had been able to overcome something he was never sure he was going to be capable of doing.

"I've won the battle up to now. It's a great feeling, I can tell you."

Zeppelin were well into the American tour by now, and it seemed appropriate to ask Plant about the long-term future of the band, particularly in view of the noisy soundings by lesser breeds who wanted them to move over and make way for youth.

Since they had gone so far since their formation in 1968, and since he was talking quite enthusiastically about their future, how did the singer see it shaping?

"We took off with so much invigorating energy in '68, and then we curbed that energy so that the whole dynamics of the band would ebb and flow, so that we wouldn't burn ourselves out musically by taking the opportunity to go hair-raisingly mad and fade a whole-lotta-loving into the sunset!", he said.

"By sitting down and taking up the challenge and realising that we were, are, and will be, capable of expanding, that can be the only hope for the future, and that's how we want to make our impression and be remembered...for constantly trying to ride the winds of change.

"And how good we were at it in the end, when it's all over, will be up to the individual to judge. I personally think we've done all right."

How did Robert see the band's fans today? Were they picking up new ones all along the line, or gaining new ones and losing old ones - what were his own observations of the audiences on this tour? He laughed and replied:-

"I'd say we have a lot of people there from the beginning or people who look as if they were! Then again, I looked behind the stage tonight, in the seats that are not readily sought after, and found a whole new breed coming up.

"Kids who've got a pirate Zeppelin T-shirt on that's much too big for them. And

then I smile. And I see our children, and kids a few steps behind them digging it, and in the end I come round to thinking that it's funny it took such a long time to bridge so many gaps, musically, y'know.

"There was, I mean, that period when there was us, alone, with so many other bands of good quality and calibre - the 'underground music' thing. Now, it doesn't mean a light, just an old cliché. Now the whole scene's wide open, and it's a matter purely of how good you are, whatever your style."

Take his own tastes, for example. He was currently studying Bulgarian folk music, especially because it was all vocal and complelty different from anything he had listened to before.

"They use quarter-tones but at the same time in their harmonies, instead of firsts, thirds, fifths and sevenths and all the conventional Western European styles of har-

mony, they use firsts and seconds.

"And I've never been trained to do anything in my life and I find it difficult to harmonise with myself on record. But I find it very inspiring to listen to stuff, like that, on the Nonsuch label from the Elektra catalogue.

"It comes straight out of the hills - it's what you might call mass singing, like village singing when a village gets together at various times of the year when they hope for this, that and the other to happen...all that we in Britain have almost lost.

"Otherwise, I'm never too far away from

never really got their just deserts for what they don't play, rather than for what they do play. I'd like to see which way Mike Heron goes next, because that album with the Reputation was good, but the Heron album was much better. He seemed a little rigid and I think he'll loosen up a little bit.

"Lots of varying styles appeal to me. There's one track over here by a group called Kansas that hasn't even come out in England, which is a big hit single here. If they have a good record company in England you should be hearing it soon and it's a good 'un - I think they're probably a bit like bands like Boston, who seem to have one good song on every album!

"And without blowing our own trumpet too much - Dave Edmunds is great (he is signed to Swansong, Zeppelin's management stable). Bit of a looney, but he's really, really good."

Because he sees so much genuine talent around, Plant seems to cast a weary, if not impatient, eye on the new wave-cum-punk movement which has gripped the nation for the past year.

First off, he said he did not feel competitive towards any of the established names, no matter what was said. "In the early days, I guess we were in competition a little, when Beck and Ronnie Wood and Rod Stewart and Mickey Waller and Nicky Hopkins were on the road, because Jeff Beck had come out of the Yardbirds and Jimmy had, and there was that interplay.

"But Jimmy's my mate, and I can tell you none of this competitiveness came from him, even though it seemed to make all the going-out-together for pleasure with other musicians an uncomfortable thing.

Robert Johnson. There's no way on this earth that I could ever find his work tiring. And then there are several things which have come up very nicely - Fleetwood Mac have taken a nice turn.

"Obviously it's not musically new, but I do like that kick-in-the-air California-sand music when it's played really well. A lot of it went sour, but Fleetwood Mac have brought something good out of it. You can never get too far away from Mick Fleetwood's drums, which is just like it used to be, the way he uses tom-tom.

"Little Feat have always intrigued me. They've

"But once we started going off, musically, on our own things settled down and we could mix easily with anyone because there's no competition. I don't mean that to sound how it probably does, big-headed, but with all good individual acts, like say the Stones, we are on our own.

"It's only on a musical level that we think of ourselves anyway. It's not who can pull the biggest crowds, 'cos we leave that to Elton, God bless him!"

Talking of crowds, Plant continued, what really was the basis of the charge by the punk bands that the dinosaur bands played to such gigantic crowds

that the magic communication twixt star and fan has been erased? This was sheer nonsense, he argued.

"It was like playing in a living room tonight at Madison Square Garden," he declared. "You could easily walk to the side of the stage, just catch somebody's eye and work to that person, like in any club. Okay, so there were 20,000 people there, but I'm willing to bet that nearly every one of them left that place happy at what they'd seen. It certainly sounded like it to me, anyway, judging from the reception they gave us.

"Let's face it, if Johnny multi-vocabulary Rotten gets his act together he'll have to take it elsewhere, leave Nottingham Boat Club behind, because they'll be too many people to get into that size of place and he'll have more people being unhappy at his lack of foresight. He'll just have to open it up bigger than that.

"He'll also have to change his act soon. It's getting a bit tiring, all that, because the dinosaur bands are still dancing."

As a trend, though, he welcomed the new wave and had taken the trouble to visit its London club, the Roxy, several weeks ago. There, he experienced Johnny Rotten, who "frightened me to death."

Plant said: "Kim Fowley's the closest I've ever seen to him, but Kim Fowley's old enough to be Johnny's dad, and Johnny's as old as me. Kim Fowley's great, one of the great innovators of all time, but he's so permanently weirded-out on such a nice level, freaky but great...anyway, I went to the Roxy and got frightened to death, but, at the same time, stood my ground for all we dinosaurs, and I saw the Damned.

"I found them very exciting, thrilling. Rat Scabies is a great drummer. He's no spring chicken either, and when I look at those eyes - well, I know that those leapers do terrible things to your eyes, but I can read the sands of time as well!

"But they're good, the Damned. If they didn't have the paint and clothing or whatever and just came along and did it, they'd probably be twice as big as they are now. But they've had to throw off the robes of the punk thing, and in doing so it's

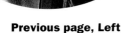

cost them time. They did that T. Rex tour, so they're obviously broken out of that melee...but anyway, they were very good.

"Other bands? I saw the group - what's that one with the 15-year-old drummer? Eater! Well, a lot of people need to go home and do their homework. I mean, I play guitar on four tracks on our albums but I wouldn't DARE play on stage.

"When all the shouting's over and it's just down to music and pulling people in who are going to sit through it, then I'll be there to see it.

"As a basic movement...it's good, but I wish the music was more original and was moving on a stage. The Stranglers, for example, sound like an English Doors pre-"LA-Woman." So that doesn't do much for me or anyone else, really.

"The intensity and the excitement I do like, because I never forget the first time I saw the Small Faces and the Who, when I was at school. It was that very thing that made me go: 'YEAH' - and I rushed to the barber's and got a French crew or whatever they were called, the right mod haircut.

"So I know what all that's about, rushing around getting a parka and immediately getting chrome side panels for your scooter, and belonging again, 'cos I was just a bit too young for the drape jackets.

"I understand all that. Everyone needs something to hang on to a little bit, on some level of mass entertainment 'when-the-work-is-done-what-are-we-gonna-do?' As long as everybody doesn't go overdosing on leapers again, it's fine.

"But I go to a lot of soccer matches" (Plant is a rabid Wolves supporter) "and I see another element of youth and that really frightens me.

"We have to make sure that the music doesn't dance hand in hand with the shed boys, because if the two elements got together, that music would do just as much harm as Chelsea losing 3-1.

"So provided the music really has got some content so that the kids really get off on it, and they wait for certain numbers to come and they really enjoy 'em - then it's worked, and it's the next step. Then it'll be only a matter of time before you're asking them, after a nine-year career, what they think of this and that.

"But you'll only be asking these punk rock bands or new wave bands, or whatever, if they vary what they're doing because there's no staying power in staying the same."

Whatever the taunts at Zeppelin as a tasteless

Previous page, Left

The Acoustic return – 'Four part harmony'

USA 1977

Previous page, Right

Robert lets loose, USA 1977

Left

Triple-neck treat for 'Ten Years Gone'

Top

Bare chested Plant – one for the ladies

Below

Drama and distortion during Page's 'Star

Spangled Banner' solo

Top

Page 'The Sorcerers Apprentice'

Below

Plant chats with Ahmet Ertegun,

co-founder of Atlantic records

Right

'The lull before the storm' –

a moment's respite for Bonzo during

acoustic interlude

macho-rock tank, it's impossible to talk to their singer without forming a real appreciation of his love for the music, which balances the slightly unacceptable doomy image of the band.

On stage he comes over with venomous bite and little real heart, and in print he's apt, perhaps, to sound glib. But in person, with the barriers down, he's what you and I would describe as "a good chap."

I put it to him that he did not sell sex on stage as did some of his contemporaries in hard rock singing, but that he relied largely on the music instead of blatant posing - surely the antithesis of what was required and expected of a true rock 'n'

roll vocalist? "I suppose that when I wear a Wolverhampton Wanderers football shirt, that's hardly sexual, but I still read a lot of things saying I'm sexually doing this and sexually looking that

on the stage.

"If any of my movements appear sexual, then they are really just accessories to the music at that point in time. I get quite heatedly involved with what's going on musically, and invariably I'm right in front of John Paul's equipment or Jimmy's. I'm concentrating on what I'm listening to and I move accordingly.

"There are movements I do all the time, regularly, but if I was going to start consciously thinking about how I was going to appear, I might begin to take myself a little too seriously in the wrong direction."

So he did not regard himself in any way as a solo attraction or personality asset to Zeppelin?

"Oh god no. I'm a member of a band. I remember reading once something John Entwhistle said about 'there go Zeppelin again, saying how they're one big happy family and they'll never break up and we've heard all this before.' But all those critics should realise that I have no vocal accelerations or any vocal movements. They are all inspired by the music around me and the knowledge that I can do it anyway and want to push it a bit farther.

"And that can only come by playing with people who surprise you. Like Jimmy's solo tonight in 'No Quarter' - it was just fantastic, very well-constructed in such a manner different from before, so that I can't help but respond differently to that.

"So that I can never see myself projecting myself as the one who does the vocals while the other three play the music."

His great stimulant was the instrumental

work of the others. "I can't see it changing dramatically either. I'm the guy who puts the words in. No part of my job is to overshadow the music.

"I'm not a symbol or anything. The only reason that could change it is if character-wise, we started drifting apart, and then to keep things together, I'd have to look elsewhere for stimulation."

And was that imminent? "Oh no, no. Bonzo and I are getting on better now than we ever have done. We've only had one fight on this tour!"

Still, he wished he could sing like Steve Marriott.

There were many moods to Led Zeppelin's music, he insisted, and he couldn't think of one single singer who was his inspiration from the same level as the heavier stuff right through to "Stairway to Heaven."

"But I could never be compared with Steve Marriott because he's too good, unfortunately! He has got the best white voice, for sheer bravado and balls. How he applies it to his career is neither here nor there, but he is the master of white contemporary blues.

"He came down to some of our rehearsals in London before this tour and to me, the two of us singing Muddy Waters songs was almost as hair-raising as our first gig.

"That's the dynamism of my vocalism which I do touch on occasionally. It's only one aspect, although Steve is the best at what he does. On the more mellow side, there are a lot of people who can control their voices in such a way that makes it pleasurable to the ear.

"At one point, Jesse Colin Young had that ability, when the Youngbloods were at their best, on 'Elephant Mountain' and things like that. Lowell George I do like, and when he sings in a subdued manner he's very good."

Since Plant's musical roots are steeped in his love of the blues, I wondered if he was especially conscious of this debt to the American heritage, and whether, as a result, he thought that the USA saw a different kind of Zeppelin performance from that enjoyed by other countries.

"Right now, America is getting a rebirth from us, like the capital letter of the first sentence of a new paragraph." But when they return to England later this year with a concert, they would be saying: look, we've been away, but this is the best we can do.

Earls Court was a peak, Alexandra Palace a disaster, with shocking sound, but right now he felt they were hitting again.

This was probably traceable to the fact that, when working away from home, they concentrated more on intense working.

"Nobody comes up and taps you on the shoulder to involve you in anything that isn't related to work when you're on the road in America. This is solely work. No side effects.

"Whereas if you're travelling from home to a gig in England, you tend to come out differently on stage, maybe you're more relaxed - but whatever, you're not wound up for work like in America, where you're in a hotel and there's all this security around us and you can definitely feel a kind of tension.

"So you get out on that stage knowing that that's the only release you can possibly have, 'cos you're here to work and WHOOSH! And after the gig, no jingle jangles or going anywhere, just back to the hotel, put on the Elmore Jones albums, and unwind that way.

"Whereas in England, working from a set base and doing a gig, going home again, it's different. Of course, if we did just an acoustic set back in England it would probably be our finest hour! Nice and mellow and gentle.

"But there's a kind of an excitement in an American audience that belongs only to an American audience, and events during the concert which you can pick up on tend to make your reactions to them, through the music, that much more adamant.

"There's a lot of mishandling of kids, for instance, by the authorities, and there are a lot of kids without manners who don't contemplate their neighbour at all - so there is all this interplay which you're very aware of.

"Whereas at an English concert it usually goes on the way it starts off. The enthusiasm builds, but it's always retained inside that composure.

"There are some towns in the Midwest where they have what's called 'festival seating', which

means no seating, the first-come-first-served effect. So you get people who've been queuing up all afternoon and they're the first in.

"By the third number, say by the time we reach 'Nobody's Fault But Mine,' there's this great milling of people and it's a bit chaotic. I have to spend about thirty minutes trying to convince these folk that it would be much better both for us and them if they had some semblance of order."

It usually worked. It was difficult not to sound tactless, because the band was, after all, playing for thousands of people who had been waiting to see them for a long time. It could have an unsettling effect on the music, too.

"Worst of all is the realisation that if the mob scenes continue, and people are milling around in a crush, somebody is going to get hurt and hit the deck.

Plant seemed aware, yet wary, of the special power invested in a rock singer of his stature. He believed it would be dangerous and irresponsible to use his personal strength as a rallying cry for whatever he wanted to be done.

Whether he was adopting this attitude because of his previously stated belief that he was "merely a musician doing the words" was difficult to perceive, but anyway I asked how he reconciled not wanting to be the front man with being the one who did the announcing, and whether he wished he was bereft of power.

"I got over that power thing about seven years ago," he answered carefully. "Everybody goes through that 'where do I stand in all this?' scene when their audiences build up from clubs to concerts to gigantic arenas and you wonder how far you should go.

"My own feeling is that you should play it very cool. A lot hangs on the balance struck, the relationship between the guy at the front of that microphone and 20,000

people, and I've learned to soft pedal very carefully.

"In the beginning you tend to try to channel their enthusiasm and build it the right way; you tend to manipulate the crowd a little bit - but it's a positive manipulation. It's not a case of let's have a riot, and f—- the cops.' You have to go the reverse, gentle way: try to take it this way, folks, because this is the best way to enjoy it.

"No, the feeling of power is a big NO in the rulebook. Anyway, on stage we rely on each other so much and if that was to come out of any one of us, the other three of us would jump on the one and say: come on, you might kid two people but you aren't kidding three!"

But did Plant concede that as the singer he held the balance of power, in the time-honoured tradition, as against, say, Jimmy Page, who ironically had the vision of Led Zeppelin and formed the band in 1968?

Well, said Robert diplomatically (for he knows when to stop talking), Zeppelin was not that kind of band. "Mick might be the Stones' leader, so you could ask him that one, but ours is er...well, more of a co-operative band. Does that answer the question?"

Not really.

"Well that's all you're gonna get! (Smiles.) "What else shall we discuss?"

How about the danger that Zeppelin were now so pre-eminently successful that they did not need to work hungrily any more? Albums selling by the million and concerts of unprecedented statistics surely blunted their need to work so hard - crowds would go bananas whatever they sang.

"I don't accept that at all. On every level, our fans seduce us to bring out the best work we can produce, and as for getting blasé just because we've made money - like the punk rock people say we have become unreachable - this isn't true, and no genuine musician who began in the clubs could get like that if his origins were pure.

"If you'd felt the magic of my mind when I first got back on that stage in Dallas six weeks back, or the magic I'm gonna feel when the next album comes out and it's the best we can do and we like it...no, we haven't got lazy or anything.

"Like I said, the only way we could have problems in this band is if our characters shape differently over the next few years and none of us has total control over the directions our individual personalities will take.

"But right from the time Jimmy Page came up to see me in the Midlands and said he was gonna form this band, way back in '68, he and I have known that we're such different characters that we're good for each other. We're totally different individuals. So no, we're not ever gonna take easy ways out."

Did he expect the band to be this big, right from the start?

"I didn't know what this big was! I mean, the Band of Joy was a little baby band and it's way back in the past, but that was always enjoyable as well. There are so many connotations to being big.

"I don't think I can yet properly relate to the magnitude of the band, although I guess it's nearly as big as sliced bread."

"It's been said that these shows are events rather than concerts, and I suppose that's true. But what's the option? I guess we must carry a little bit of a legend with us, and you don't have to over-try, or it will come over clinical, clear-cut and jumpy.

"We have to bring out our very best all the time, because kids have a right to expect that, but we don't have to produce it in a stiff-upper-lip way or it comes out the wrong kind of tight.

"It's got to be Tight But Loose. That's probably the title of the next album."

When would that appear? "We haven't even started thinking about it constructively yet. We're hoping to do a summer show and make a mark on England and maybe we'll be working on the album in the autumn.

"Then again, after this marathon American tour we might all want to go home and lie horizontal for a while, or lean against the apple tree."

Previous page, Left

Destroyers - centrestage. An evening with Led Zeppelin

Previous page, Right

(Top) Page cools off between songs,

(Below) John Bonham 'A roar of approval'

Left

Led Zeppelin – Four badge holders only

Below

'The Mighty Arms of Atlas' - Achilles Last Stand

Out of the Shadows

Little was heard of Led Zeppelin in the early months of the year, and many continued to speculate that they had broken up for good, despite Page insisting in a series of press interviews that they were simply waiting for the bereaved Robert Plant to once again feel ready to participate. Eventually, they regrouped to rehearse again halfway through the year, and Plant eased himself back into performing mode via some unprepublicised sit-in gigs, at first with local pub groups near his home, and then in impromptu fashion with the likes of Dave Edmunds and Dr Feelgood (the latter while he was on holiday in Ibiza!). Eventually, at the very end of the year, following six weeks of writing and rehearsal in London, the reunited Zeppelin travelled to Sweden, at the invitation of Abba, to record at the latter group's new Polar Studios in Stockholm, and in three weeks of intensive sessions, most of a new album was completed.

Mr Page wishes to announce...that he is perfectly normal

No splits, no bad karma, no heaviness. Just a plain , ordinary rock'n'roller at heart. Angie Errigo relays the message.

December 3

Originally, I toyed with the idea of kicking off my contribution to "Dialogues with Jimmy Page" with a flashy intellectual quotation from George Eliot's Daniel Deronda about what a bruise it is to meet an idealised person and be confronted with their inevitable normalness.

This was supposed to suggest to you that I'm really quite intelligent, so that when you got to the meat and potatoes of the interview you wouldn't be so quick to notice how timidly I held up my end of things.

Then I decided not to get too cute.

What happened, simply, was that after years of imagining that, given the opportunity, I could extract from the chosen victim the definitive personality profile, I was outsmarted.

Sterner stuff than I have been stymied by the Professional Interviewee.

While a lot of these rock star fellows are not all that sharp in the verbal department, or can be tricked into spilling beans by excessive liquid refreshment or cunning strategy, there are those who give interviews because they have something they want to say and, having said it, cannot be induced to drop their guard and muse aloud on their fears and foibles. Mick Jagger is notably such a one.

He has nothing on Jimmy Page.

Summoned at last into the presence, the ambition of wrestling him into a corner, overpowering him and stomping on his chest in stilettos until he

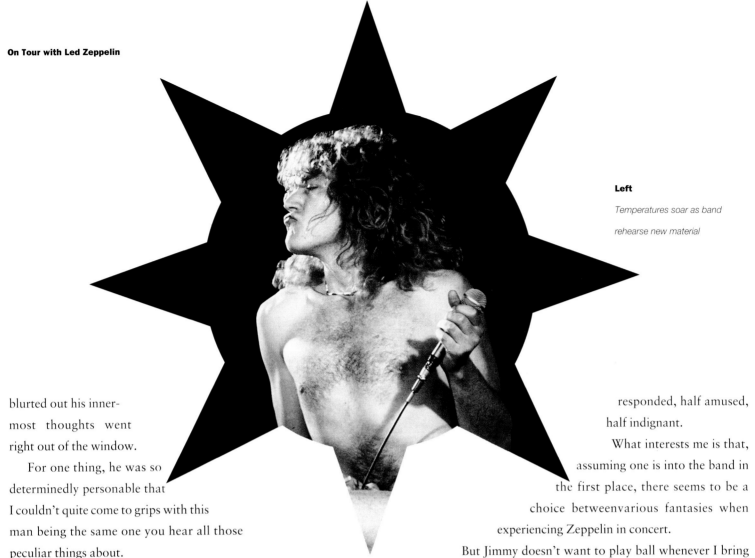

blurted out his inner-most thoughts went right out of the window.

For one thing, he was so determinedly personable that I couldn't quite come to grips with this man being the same one you hear all those peculiar things about.

What about all this awe and terror bit in his image, then?

"Well, I felt overawed when I met Elvis Presley – I've gotta own up – and whenever I've met any of the sort of people I felt were great heroes. It's natural. But after five minutes, if the people are reasonably human, if they're not trying to send you up or something, you end up having a normal conversation."

Butter wouldn't melt in his mouth, eh? But the whole Zeppelin schtick, and the persona of Jimmy Page as its architect, has been so heavily inlaid and encrusted with fantasy and fascination as to make him a many-faced enigma, consciously or not.

"What I really want to know about you is what it's like to be the real you," I told him.

"Well, I'm the real me all the time," he responded, half amused, half indignant.

What interests me is that, assuming one is into the band in the first place, there seems to be a choice betweenvarious fantasies when experiencing Zeppelin in concert.

But Jimmy doesn't want to play ball whenever I bring up this kind of thing, maintaining a stubborn but preictable "I'm just a rock and roller at heart!" line.

But don't you feel affected by being so many things to so many people and by all the fantasies your audiences project on to you?

And what about all the more obsessive goofs who regularly spring out of Swan-Song's morning post with their Page-centred religious and occult bees-in-the-bonnet?

It doesn't seem to interest him. "I've made a point of not getting into all that because it can get really pretentious," he says placidly.

Foiled again.

Having lost my grip I let him talk about what he wanted. (This resulted in a 20,000 word transcript recounting the intimate details of the wiring up of his new recording desk. The book comes out next year.)

Back into the realms of sensationalism. For Page the real purpose of the interview was to dispel rumours.

His first concern was to deny any Zeppelin split and to blast the musical press for its insensitivity in speculating on Robert Plant's plans while he wants to remain in privacy

Right

Peter Grant, the fifth

member of Led Zeppelin.

Grant, assisted by Richard

Cole, enhanced the groups

progress and reputation,

with a unique style of

management

Overleaf

Robert Plant

with his family after his young son's death.

"There's no question of the thing splitting up. I know Robert wants to work again."

I asked what other things have been put about that he wanted to straighten out and he said: "You tell me," but as I hesitantly pulled out a variety of Loose Talk he got pretty sore.

One thing is that supposedly Robert doesn't want anything to do with Jimmy any more, and before I could finish he asked with astonishment, "Why's that?"

Well, er, they do say that he seems to have been the lightning rod for a lot of - you'll pardon the expression -bad karma.

This causes a minor explosion. "What do you mean by karma? It's not karma at all, I don't see how the band would merit a karmic attack.

"All I or we have attempted to do is to go out and really have a good time and please people at the same time. I always thought I was very fortunate through that, 'cause I can't think of anything better than doing what you really want to do and seeing just a mass of smiles. That's Utopia.

"Everybody in the band is really determined to do the best for themselves and the people who've followed us up to now without bullshitting around. I just don't see how there could be a bad karma or whatever.

"I think it's just bad coincidence. Okay, one may say there's no such thing as coincidence, but I really feel that."

Well, there have been whispers, nevertheless, that perhaps an unfortunate association with Page, specifically something like the upset with occult film-maker Kenneth Anger, led to him or somebody else putting the whammy on the band.

"It just really upset me, that, because I really did think that he (Anger) was an avatar at one point.

"Sure enough, he really is good when it comes down to his statement on celluloid. But you can never know, I mean, it's like Blake, Einstein, any of these people, you never really know what they're going through.

"Some of the things that manifested on his personal life just totally perplexed me. I can't account for the lunatic fringe."

Okay, then there are the conflicting accounts of how heavy Zeppelins's big boys, Peter Grant and Richard Cole, really are in handling the band's business affairs. (When this came up I couldn't but help getting the heebie-jeebies due to Cole's presence behind me).

Page wasn't present at the well-publicised backstage fight in San Francisco, to cite a particular episode, but he's prepared to back up Grant and John Bonham.

According to him the audience had already been getting a bad time from brutish bouncers all day, and the eventual confrontation came after Grant's little boy was mishandled.

"I'll tell you, there was a whole team of guys there with sand in their gloves. It was a very, very hairy scene.

"I've had brushes with Bill Graham in the past. I'll give you an example. It was the Fillmore East where we really broke, and the whole name and news of the group spread like wildfire through the States from there. Obviously, on the return we were excited to be back and really wanted to do our best.

"Now, when we got there it was in the afternoon and I went in with the road manager 'cause we wanted to cart the gear in then, and Graham was playing basketball. I remember going up to him - he didn't seem to be doing anything at the time, he seemed like the referee - and I said, 'Hi Bill, it's really good to see you. Can we bring the gear in now?'

"And he said, 'don't you fucking get in here, you mother-fuckers' and all this real abuse. It was just like he exploded.

"I was really brought down because we really built ourselves up to going back.

"Then later he apologised. What I mean is, he's a pendulum."

There is still one story doing the rounds that one of the bouncers involved died later, I told him.

"That's nonsense! Listen, if we'd killed anybody we'd be bloody in prison. It's ridiculous. It was just a civil case. If somebody hits you and you hit them back it's self-defence, innit?

"It's just another thing that got blown up. I don't want to say too much about it."

In a less inflammatory vein, Jimmy Page tales are rife.

One of the most persistent is that if Zeppelin did split, he'd be willing to do service with the Stones if Keith got screwed. Is that nonsense too?

"Well, I've played with Ronnie Wood and Keith and we always have a good time. But it's only jamming.

"I was upset with that because it looked like it was a stab in the back on Keith, and I really like

and respect him."

Another current favourite is the one about Pagey enjoying a spot of television viewing, suddenly seeing UFOs on the screen, grabbing his toothbrush and tearing off to Cairo, presumably for a rendezvous with little green men. (This had been reported in NME by Nick Kent.)

"That's because somebody didn't really read what I'd said, and they were just being bloody stupid.

"I was going to go to Cairo on the tour break and I was tossing up whether or not to go. And there was this TV programme hosted by Omar Sharif about the mysteries of the pyramids. And they showed this old footage of the pyramids with a zeppelin flying in and I thought, 'That's it! I'll definitely go.' It seemed to be such a strange coincidence that that bit of footage should be there on the day I was thinking about it.

"But UFOs, that's just the usual sort of nonsense that goes on."

"I'm totally committed to music. There's no point in trying to deny it within myself. It's the only thing I'm any good at. And I'm not a natural player or anything like that. It's all down to work"

Risking one final upset, I bring up the criticisms of SwanSong.

"The only criticisms that have gone down about SwanSong are from Jake Riviera, who seems to be using anything as a springboard to get his name out. I don't really understand all that thing with Nick Lowe.

"Lowe is as sweet as apple pie to your face; that's all I really need to say about him."

What about complaints that Peter Grant doesn't have time for anyone on the label besides Zeppelin and Bad Company?

"Well, there is one awkward situation with the label, which is that a lot of folk come along and seem to think that Peter Grant is going to be able to do everything for them. It's just one of those unfortunate things that he's there and they respect him, but he just doesn't want to know. He's got too much on his plate.

"We've had a bit of a shake-up in the record department. After having gone through two label managers we've found out we can do it better ourselves."

I decided to drop the gossip probe at this stage. The thankless task of scrutinising the interior of the Zeppelin hierarchy and the Swansong structure can go to a tough investigative reporter.

The future of Led Zeppelin itself is obviously very much on Page's mind.

"I do feel it's time to do some really major, meaty work."

Is the band a stable thing in his life that he has come to depend on?

"Well, I get such a charge from playing with everybody. It became so apparent on the last tour that it was something which I really needed."

Gigging in Britain after an enforced two-and-a-half years, is, he says, definitely a major priority.

"If we hadn't had the awful end on this last tour everyone would have been in the frame of mind to bring over everything that we had in America because we were so knocked out with the show and the presentation.

"It was a great relief and release to be able to get back on stage and work. Obviously the first five gigs were rusty, but the audience just acted like 'Whoo, great to see you back'.

"I must admit I didn't know whether I was capable of playing for three-and-a-half hours. You could bullshit for an hour, but you can't bullshit for three-and-a-half hours or people are going to get bored. And they didn't - the enthusiasm was building all the time.

"We had a good programme which covered everything, and we had worked very hard on the environmental aspect of it. You could see the effects like the laser pyramid from a mile away.

"In the really massive places we used videos, which is only fair, really. 'Cause I remember going to Wembley to see Crosby, Stills, Nash and Young and I thought it was the roadies on stage at first.

"When we did Earls Court we were so determined to do the same sort of show and more than what we'd been doing in America that in the end we came out of it with just a few hundred pounds over the five days; but it didn't matter because the vibe was so electrifying."

Throughout the conversation, Page's preoccupation with the work he's engaged in at home is most evident. How exasperating a musician like this can be. Every time you try to get sociological he will talk about music. (What a B.O.F. - Ed.)

"I've been setting up a studio at home which is so advanced that there's one bit which is still in the laboratories having tests made on it.

"Basically it's a computerised desk with a memory bank. There are automated desks around now which just do the volume and the level, but this does every single thing on the board.

"I've been learning how to use it. It's taken a bloody long time; the structural part of it was started before last Christmas and the wiring-up's been two solid months. But anyway, it's playing back now and I've started attempting to do a bit of recording on it.

"I dreamt of having a studio years and years back, before the group even started. But I always wanted to have one which wouldn't go out of date in a year.

"Now this thing should last until they do digital recording. I don't want to get too technical,

but what it does is, as you build up your mix track by track and you get your balance and equalisation and all the rest of it, it's logging it all the time and playing it back exactly as you've programmed it.

"When you finally build up the mix, if you find that the voice wasn't loud enough or something like that, you can just put the track into Rewrite and nothing else changes. It stays constant while you make your alterations.

"And you can put down six or eight alternative mixes and then go into those and take the best bits if you want to.

"The possibilities are immense. It allows you to work on your own without an engineer, and anyone who's familiar with 24-track knows how many hands are usually needed to get it right."

With a slightly guilty laugh he adds that he won't have to ring up any more engineers in the middle of the night to come and help him.

Part of this recording activity includes work on the chronological live album Page is compiling from tapes of the band from 1969 onwards.

"I'm working on it slowly because I get into that and it's really good academic practice. Then I'll get sidetracked and want to write something."

Also in his hands is one of the new Roland guitar synthesisers, which he says is amazing.

"It takes over from the keyboard; it's just programmed by the guitar, and it also plays chords.

"I've been working on all these things - new ideas and sounds. And I've got like two-and-a-half years of demo stuff to merge in with all this new work. It's all very good at the moment, because as I say, it's like the pre-Zeppelin dream.

"So there's all that - apart from all these things like holidays people keep going on about," he mutters to himself.

An interesting dichotomy emerges from discussing his own musical ambitions in contrast to the merits he appreciates in the New Wave.

"When I heard it it seemed like adrenalin music, so high-powered, and I thought it was amazing, especially The Damned.

Right

A rare group shot at Bray Studios,

Berkshire prior to Knebworth Festival

appearances

"It was very much like mantra music; they weren't altering the tempo at all, just keeping it really, really intense.

"But the ones who want to stick to the original format are probably getting a bit hackneyed now.

"It'll be interesting to see how they do develop, keeping that raw earthiness."

But at the same time he admits to feeling frustration over the failure of the rock and roll culture to throw up any people he regards as real geniuses on a par with the beacons of 'straight' classical symphonic music.

"That's what really upsets me about rock. All the barriers are opened up, all the classification is gone really, and you find people amalgamating this, that and the other music together, and yet there doesn't seem to be anything that's really important without being pretentious. All those really strong melodies like Wagner's - there just isn't anybody.

"So maybe it's just destined to be street music and social comment. Which makes it art, because an artist is somebody who, ideally, reflects his environment."

He almost hesitantly describes some of his work in progress.

"There are two pieces which are heavily orchestrated. One thing might sound odd, but the guitars are doing everything, taking over the string part and the brass part. They are heavily treated with synthesisers and effects.

"I've done a few bits of orchestration on the records up to now, but nothing really long or substantial. This is something entirely different.

"One thing I'm doing is like a cross between flamenco and modern classical on the acoustic with electric parts that keep coming in and fading out again, so that there are four totally different, but related, sections coming in.

"It's not quite the same as symphonic stuff. I don't keep going back to a theme, but it's got that sort of thickness to it. There are lots of counter-melodies and things.

"Now when you start talking like that a lot of people I know go, 'Oh dear, well that's not what's really happening'. But I was very interested to notice that when The Damned split Rat Scabies was saying, 'We were trying to stretch out'. That's it, it's a matter of change.

"A lot of people can't handle that, they just want to fit you into one bag and hope that you're going to stay there all the time."

How far do these aspirations and plans fit in with Zeppelin's future and Page's beyond that?

"I've always had a little plan of what I'd like to do, and it's materialising a lot slower than the way I initially intended.

"But it still goes hand-in-hand with the band. Whatever I'm going to do, it's only going to be a fourth of that.

"I'm totally committed to music. There's no point in trying to deny it within myself. It's the only thing I'm any good at. And I'm not a natural player or anything like that. It's all down to work.

"But I really enjoy the recorded sound and messing around getting unusual combinations. Most people would find it very boring, but I get as much buzz out of that as a motorcyclist gets out of his motorcycle."

Maybe this has turned out to be more of a

personality inventory than I thought. Shrinks say that the only really happy people are those who are strongly motivated by their work. So is Jimmy Page happy?

"I'd never ever be happy. The only time I felt - oh no, I won't say the only time - but you know I get very enthusiastic and excited over something that's being written out of nowhere.

"Obviously there are a lot of things one has to come up against which you really hate. But I could never retire because it's so fascinating; you never know what's coming next. It's a challenge, a mystery. It's like dancing on the edge of a precipice..."

Renaissance

For the first time in two years, Led Zeppelin played live again, with two headlining British dates at the Knebworth Festival in August. The band played crowd-driving three-hour sets on each date, with all the paraphenalia of lasers, giant video screens and so on, which they had used during their gruelling 1977 United States mega-trek. The release of In Through The Out Door, the album recorded at the end of the previous year in Sweden, followed immediately after these gigs, and even in a UK where the charts were jointly gripped by the onslaught of New Wave punk records and Disco music, it reached the premier slot. Their unstopable success on the other side of the Atlantic was even more spectacular: in almost two months at the top of the charts, the album pulled in all the existing Led Zeppelin back-catalogue into the charts too, giving the band nine LPs among the 200 best-sellers. At the very end of the year, the group members (Jimmy Page excepted) played live once again, when they took part in the UNICEF Rock For Kampuchea concerts at London's Hammersmith Odeon, playing Paul McCartney's Rockestra.

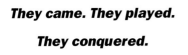

They came. They played.

They conquered.

Then they vanished, while a whole

new species sprang up to populate

the rock universe.

Now Led Zeppelin return, and want

their old room back.

Jimmy Page waves the rent book.

Smiling men with bad reputations

Chris Salewicz,   August 4th 1979

Of all the old superfart bands it is certainly Led Zeppelin who have been and still are the most reviled by the New Wave.

Whatever jerk-off socialite absurdities Jagger may have got himself into, The Rolling Stones have at least always had one of the prime punk archetypes in Keith Richards. The Who, meanwhile, have the ever-perceptive Townshend, a man who appears to have gone through something of a personal rejuventation that seems to be a direct result of his encounters with Punk.

For whatever reasons, though, the manner in which Led Zeppelin have consistently presented themselves has made the band's name synonymous with gratuitous excess. Even the almost equally guilty Pink Floyd have at least had the decency and sensitivity not to quit these shores just for the sake of saving money.

Don't sell your soul for silver and gold, as Lee Perry once said. If rock'n'roll is essentially an all-encompassing roots culture, then obviously any musician who isolates himself away in some anal retentive tax exile life-style is neither  responding to his obligations nor in harmony with those roots. Also, his initial purpose and motivation must be doubted.

The Clash's Paul Simenon summed up pretty well the total lack of respect that the new bands feel towards Zeppelin. "Led Zeppelin??? I don't need to hear the music - all I have to do is look at one of their album covers and I feel like throwing up!"

In some ways part of the reason for the venomous loathing directed at the band is not just because they've let themselves down, but also because you know damn well that Jimmy Page at least - like many of the new Punk icons a former art student - certainly

knows better.

"I've read about many records which are supposed to have turned me on to play rock'n'roll," the guitarist told New York's Trouser Press in September 1977, "but it was 'Baby, Let's Play House' by Presley...I heard that record and I wanted to be part of it; I knew something was going on. I heard the acoustic guitar, slap bass and electric guitar -three instruments and a voice - and they generated so much energy I had to be part of it. That's when I started."

Yet, in the same way that the death of the original, classic rock'n'roll punk the previous month to the publication of that article could have been seen as a serious warning of the false paths and box canyons into which Babylon could misroute rock'n'rollers, it also appeared at the time that perhaps the whole mighty edifice which Led Zeppelin had

created itself to be was starting to crumble away as inevitably as the Malibu Beach Colony will one day slide into the Pacific Ocean.

By the middle of the year when the two sevens clashed, the belief that the whole Led Zeppelin operation had got it all more than a little bit wrong appeared to be being backed up by concrete facts. The band appeared to be in a state of crisis. In artistic terms they seemed to have reached an absolute nadir. Following the turgid 'Presence' LP released in the Spring of the previous year there'd

the outset. It was to have been the band's first live work since 1975 when vocalist Robert Plant had been severely injured in a car smash on the Greek island of Rhodes during a year of British tax exile. It was ominous then that the first dates were cancelled when Plant developed a throat infection.

Jimmy Page himself was also believed not to be in a good state, an assumption fuelled by the news that the full time services of a doctor were being employed to care for the guitar hero. Now Page denies that the medic was there to look after him alone - "We had a doctor to look after all of us, period. It was a bloody long tour" - with the same ease that he dismisses reports of his having been wheeled around between gigs in a wheel-chair - "I may have done that for a laugh -not seriously. No, no. That wasn't happening at all."

In addition, manager Peter Grant was said to be severely depressed following a divorce. Matters appeared to reach what seemed to be an inevitably unpleasant culmination when, following a Bill Graham-promoted San Francisco gig, one of the promoter's security men was badly beaten up by Grant, drummer John Bonham and one John Bindon, a Zeppelin employee.

If some form of near-tragedy during the tour had seemed unavoidable, however, it was yet to wreak its worst toll. This happened some two weeks later when Robert Plant's five-year-old son died of a sudden mystery virus infection and the tour was abandoned whilst the grief-stricken singer flew home.

Now, of course, all these incidents may be seen as random happenings, as the chance intervention of fate. However, if you believe that you create your own fate and that human beings do not exist in isolation from one another and from the universe but are

then been, six months later, the critically lambasted 'The Song Remains The Same' film and double soundtrack album. Even this emphasis on double records - suggested attempts to milk their own market for all it was worth whilst fighting a rearguard action to forestall an inevitable end.

Perhaps more to the point, though, a general atmosphere of personal doom and gloom appeared to surround the once apparently invincible Zeppelin. The lengthy US tour undertaken by the outfit in the Spring of '77 seemed ill-fated from

part of a far greater, interacting scheme in which actions and activities scheme in which actions and activities of the past create those of the future, then all this begins to look rather different.

Certainly, Jimmy Page's interests in the occult suggest that he should believe in such a cosmic overview. Indeed, there are those who would claim that it is solely down to Page's interests in these matters that such as tragic atmosphere has surrounded Led Zep-

pelin in its latter years. Personally, though, I don't think that Jimmy Page has inked a pact with Satan. To think like that is mere superstition - and that's taking into account certain rumours which have floated about the music business the past 18 months or so that there are even certain members of the Zeppelin entourage themselves who lay the blame for these assorted misfortunes on Page's fascination with Aleister Crowley.

When it comes down to it, though, I don't really think that there's been some clear-cut metaphysical holy war of good and evil waged on the rock'n'roll boards the band has been treading the past ten years. In fact, it's probably that outside interest which has kept the guitarist's head relatively together during the most successful years of the band. The occult, after all, is concerned with knowledge and plumbing one's own mystic depths for certain truths that are beneficial to the whole of humanity. Yes, of course, it can be used in a malevolent manner, but to view all occult activity as the work of the Devil is a red herring laid down by Babylon and therefore is the work of the tricky Devil himself.

I think, though, that Jimmy Page is very confused. His confusion doesn't spring from his occult interests but, I feel, from the very nature of Led Zeppelin itself and his position with regard to the band of which he is undoubtably the leader. Indeed, when we met last Friday evening in the SwanSong offices on the hottest day of the year, it became glaringly obvious that Jimmy Page was

Previous page, Left

Robert Plant stuns the crowd at

the 1979 Knebworth Festival

Previous page, Right

The remarkable spectacle

of a huge video-image back-

drop of Jimmy Page, dwarfing

the usually larger-than-life

Robert Plant

Left

The Final Homecoming.

400,000 fans witnessed Led

Zeppelin's final UK concerts at

Knebworth Park, Hertfordshire

over two Saturdays in August

Below

Page – The guitar hero for

future generations

totally comfortable, and, at times, positively exhilarated when talking about these extra-curricular acitivities.

It was noticeable, however, that when the conversation changed to the subject of his band he appeared frequently to find eye contact exceptionally awkward. Now, it's quite possible to blame that on the fact that in the isolated, self-enclosed existence in which Jimmy Page dwells he probably doesn't have that much verbal interchange with people outside his own sphere. Also, like many musicians who're far more at ease when living out their fantasies onstage, he may well be slightly nervous. Mind you, although a hermetic, fairly newsless lifestyle is part of the whole Led Zeppelin problem anyway, Page's behaviour does suggest that he is not always totally convinced by his arguments - and Page is adept in the art of being a media salesman for his band whilst at the same time revealing little about himself; check how many times the word "Knebworth" gets men-

tioned. It's the very nature of Led Zeppelin itself that is the problem. Let's not mince words, it's always been regarded as a "heavy" operation. There has been a slightly odd vibe about it.

Now, of course, part of the nature of rock'n'roll is the manner in which it allows people involved with it to live out their childhood Cowboy & Indian fantasies. So I don't know whether Peter Grant really is a figure from the fringes of the underworld or whether he just enjoys people thinking he is. I suppose it doesn't really matter (though in a way it does) because I've no doubt, as

Page himself comments later on, that certain of the behind-the-scenes music industry figures with whom he has to deal, particularly in the States, actually are dodgy characters. So maybe it gives him an edge over them. (Unless they're also all just living out their fantasies - in which case it all gets a bit complicated and self-perpetuating, and a bit pointless too.)

"The whole point of the bit in The Song Remains The Same film," Page tells me when I ask him about this, "where Peter plays a gangster was just to send up all that and show how it was just a joke anyway."

Nevertheless, I counter, there was the slight problem with the security guy in San Francisco. There's certainly concern in his voice when he replies "I didn't see it, you know, so I can't say exactly what happened. There were no million dollar law-suits put out on me, y'know.

"But," he continues, "you must remember that Bill Graham has a very heavy reputation, that all his security people have a reputation for heaviness. As for Peter...Well, he's a very big guy and, if people are coming up to him all the time and calling him a bastard and telling him to piss off to his face, then he's probably going to react accordingly."

Alright, fair enough. But let's not forget that John Bindon is currently in Brixton, either awaiting or serving a sentence for a subsequently committed manslaughter - an incident which wasn't

connected in any way with Led Zeppelin. Once again, judging from his reply to being reminded of this, there's no doubt that this genuinely troubles Page, much more out of real concern for Bindon, I feel, than for any unhappiness about him being linked with Zeppelin. It's a pity I forgot at the time, but I'd like to have also got his reaction to Nick Kent's claim that John Bonham once threw a drink over the hapless writer for a negative review.

But that's by the bye, I suppose. it seems more important to tell the guitarist that, whether he's aware of this or not, an oft-expressed opinion on Led Zeppelin has been that the problems Robert Plant has faced have been something of a kharmic backlash that Plant, as the most accessible and open band member, has had directed towards him.

Page seems very shocked by this. "I don't think that's so," he replies slowly, almost as though slightly dazed, "if what we were doing was really evil then...then I suppose we'd just put out lots of records and try and make loads of money...I hope that's not so."

Sometime about the middle of last Friday morning I'd had a call from the SwanSong press office. Could I arrive maybe an hour before the interview was due to begin? That way I could be given an earful of the new Zep waxing. I can't pretend the idea exactly thrilled me to the bones, especially in the light of the last studio album 'Presence', which I find utterly unenjoyable. If I felt the same way about the new, as yet untitled, LP it could mean a chilly start to an interview.

By lunchtime, however, this potentially awkward situation had been resolved by Jimmy Page himself. A further phonecall passed on the information that the guitarist felt it pointless for me to hear the record as it was, apparently, "a separate entity" - from what I'm not certain. Obviously it did cross my mind that maybe he was thinking the same way as myself and saw little gain in the songs being numbered some time before the record was even released.

Perhaps predictably, when the record did come to be mentioned he was full of enthusiasm for it. The titles of the new numbers are: Side 1 - 'In The Evening', 'South Bound Suarez', 'Hot Dog'; Side 2 - 'Carouselambra', 'All My Love', 'I'm Gonna Crawl'. The Knebworth bashes will feature "at least two songs from the new album plus several numbers from previous LPs that haven't been performed live in the past." What can I say?

I was also asked for some idea of the sort of questions I'd be asking. As I was at that time deciding on these for myself I couldn't really help out there. Besides, would this not have detracted for the natural spontaneity of the occasion? I was, however, informed that questions about the death of Plant's son and about Aleister Crowley were strictly taboo. This did not augur particularly well, especially when, whilst waiting for the assistant editor chap from the MM to finish his rap with Jim, photographer Adrian Boot emerged from that session to inform Pennie and myself that Page was "doing a Chuck Berry" and ignoring most of Watt's questions. The guitarist was also apparently none to happy about Boot's snapping needs.

In the event, of course, Page gave Pennie plenty of pix-taking time prior to our encounter.

Also, as far as my interview went, Page and I just starting taking it conversationally (but not before he made a rapid attempt to flog Knebworth) rather than adhering to any strict question and answer form. This state of affairs lasted for much of the whole interview.

Page was drinking pints of lager from a straight plastic glass and chainsmoking Marlboros. So was I. It was probably down to a combinatin of the booze and the hot weather, but the conversation quickly became very speedy. Maybe we were also blocked on the carbon monoxide fumes wafting in through the open window from the early evening rush-hour traffic three floors below on the Kings Road.

What with the roar of London Transport Roadmasters stopping just past the offices and the constant rumble of jets on their way to Heathrow overhead, it was often hard for either of us to make out what the other was saying. Though his enunciation is very clear indeed, Jimmy Page's soft Surrey accent - the family business is Page Motors in Epsom - makes him perhaps the most quietly spoken interviewee I've ever come across. Even so, I was pleased that he didn't pull the slumped-out whispering wimp number that I'm told is one of his favourite interview techniques. Not once, I think, did he lean back on the couch on which he was seated next to the window.

No doubt exacerbated by the booze intake - Jim is fond of the odd tipple, I'm told - perspiration poured off of his forehead in large drops, frequently lodging for a few moments in his close-to-shoulder length hair. Coupled with the collarless striped white shirt he wore, he didn't

look very different at all from when in the late '60s he laid down the ground rules for the classic pre-Raphaelite, faint androgynous British rock star. He actually looked younger that when I'd encountered him a couple of years back. Only worry lines around his eyes gave any indication of his age.

The Selling of Knebworth began right from the very onset. I don't think you really like doing interviews, do you, I ask? "Well, (laughs) it depends. I don't mind if the questions are alright."

You look incredibly well.

"Well, I'm looking forward to...to Knebworth, actually. We've done a lot of rehears-

ing and checked things out. We've actually been down there and worked things out in relation to the actual site."

It must seem odd with it being such a long time since you've played onstage.

"Well, it did at first...But then again it's like a natural amphitheatre, so I should imagine it's actually quite a good gig to be at. I went to Black-

States, and also in Germany from where he'd just returned, then we can get onto this matter of Punk Rock and the New Wave without too much discomfort.

Instead, though, Page mentions his surprise that Dylan had played in Nuremberg. "I couldn't believe him doing that. They played the place where they had all the big rallies. He must have come out of there feeling very strange. I know I would and I'm not even Jewish."

He hasn't heard of Dylan's conversion to Christianity. "Oh, that's very interesting. Especially after that Nuremberg thing. When did that happen? Quite recently?"

Oh, about six months or so ago, I think.

"We met his mum once, actually," Page tells me, "it was about the third tour and we were in Miami, and this typical Miami woman comes up with the spectacles and tinted hair bit and she says 'Oh, I hear you're a group. My son's a singer. You've probably heard of him - Bobby Dylan. He's a good lad,' she said.

"The strangest thing she said of all was that he always goes back to his...You know, the school turn-out when they got their degrees and things. He always goes back to that...Which is obviously a side of Dylan that many people would be actually shocked about. He's probably very orthodox in some areas where you expect him to be very bizarre and anarchistic."

Logically, I suppose, the matter of meeting Dylan at a reggae gig leads to matters Rastafarian.

"Yeah, it's very interesting: the lost Tribe Of Israel and all that. It was at the time when Haile Selassie died that I wondered 'What's going to

bushe, but that was bit of a sea of bodies. But it was great to see Dylan."

Phew, that was close. The Zim to the rescue. At least we can talk about Bob Dylan for a while. This might be handy. Maybe if I mention to Jim that I met Dylan last year when he went to an Alton Ellis gig at the 100 Club and that he told me how he preferred the vibe of England to that in the

happen now?' because there is this big thing that
he's invincible and that he would never die but
obviously," he chuckles, "he could give up his
bodily form if he wanted to - that was the
inevitable loophole.

"But it is fascinating."

We talk about Egypt for a minute or two.
Page's trip to Cairo had, indeed, been the subject
of some quite splendid rumours. On the first leg,
I think it was, of that last ill-fated Led Zeppelin
US tour it was said that one night he'd been
watching TV when the screen became filled with
flashing lines. Immediately, so the tale went, he
cancelled the next dates and flew off to Egypt.
The conversation didn't lead into my mentioning
that and, besides, I'm fairly certain I once read a
fairly thorough refutation by the guitartist of that
story.

Thoughts of Cairo seem to make Page feel
very happy. "I didn't want to come home," he
smiles, "it was so good. I didn't go for long
enough, though. I went at the end of an American
tour and with every day I was there family ties in
England were pulling more strongly, I just
thought, 'oh, I'll be back soon' and haven't made
it yet. I'd certainly like to see The Valley Of The
Kings near Luxor.

"I haven't been to many Arab countries, but
I've been to Morocco and there and in other hot
countries there's this constant hub-bub, but in
Egypt it's just so tranquil. It really is quite an
experience. Let alone the pyramids.

Equinox, the Kensington occult bookshop
that Page owned and which specialised in the
works of Aleister Crowley, is closed these days.

Far Left

The visual highlight of the performance was the innovative use of a Ramport/Holco Krypton laser show during Jimmy Page's violin bow guitar solo

Left

John Bonham – Man of Steel – employed phased tympanis to enhance his thunderous drum sound

The lease expired and, besides, "it obviously wasn't going to run the way it should without some drastic business changes and I didn't really want to have to agree to all that. I basically just wanted the shop to be the nucleus, that's all."

His interests in the occult haven't in any way diminished, however. "I'm still very interested. I still read a lot of literature on it."

And so, boys and girls, we come to that section of the interview when we talk to Jimmy Page about New Wave music. Even though he seems to consider Dire Straits a New Wave band, Page is perfectly aware that there are punk bands and punk bands who aren't really punk bands. He has heard the Clash and appears to rather like them. He warms very much to the mention of Ian Dury. "Yeah, he really imparts such a really great feeling, doesn't he? Makes you feel so good. That was certainly the first thing that struck me about New Wave music – that it was sheer adrenalin that was pouring out. Real energy tearing to get out."

But how did the beat group Led Zeppelin relate to it? They were presumably aware of what was going on. I remember Page and Plant going down

the Roxy to check out The Damned once.

"We were aware of it," he nods, "but it's not…I mean music is like a 360 degree circle from which some people may drop out to let others come in. And there are obvious examples of that – say, the feeling Free generated and which was replaced by Bad Company. Also, the raw blues, going back to the early Fleetwood Mac days. Well, now you have George Thorogood. And Herman's Hermits are replaced by the Bay City Rollers.

"Bands like us and – I hate to say it but – The Floyd…we're off in our own little bits. It's always open for anybody who's really raw and earthy and who makes sheer rock'n'roll music. Even though much of the New Wave had the political content…I mean, The Damned – I was absolutely amazed by the power that was coming out of them. Though they didn't really fit into the New Wave movement as such.

"Nevertheless, these are categories. But it's all relative; anyone who plays good music and is expressing themselves with an instrument or on vocals has got something to say. It just depends whether you can relate to them or not. And that depends on whether your musical tastes are narrow or very broad."

And certainly from what you're saying you would claim to relate to New Wave…

"Yes. But I can also relate to classical music – and you won't get them saying that…"

Oh, don't count on it, I think you'd be very surprised.

"Oh…well…good…well, they ought to."

I think if you went round to places of a few punk musicians you'd be very surprised by the width of listening materials you'd come across...

But equally, and I think it must be said, of all the Old Fart bands certainly Led Zeppelin, for whatever reasons, are the most loathed...

"Really???" Jimmy Page sounds quite startled.

Ghosts Of Progressive Rock Past
Paul Morely, August 11 1979

The sixth Annual Knebworth Park Festival was like a ghost of those simpler, smoother, days of progressive rock, ironically saved only by the nervous energy and genuine amazed-to-be-there vitality of the accepted Holy Ghosts themselves, Led Zeppelin.

And yet the only moments that connected the rock'n'roll of Knebworth with the rock'n'roll of Final Solution, or the rock'n'roll of The Undertones playing The Marquee that night (and things like liberation and outrage, abandon and passion) were during those periods when Led Zeppelin kept within the narrow range of their true expertise and played some of the most exhilarating music that I've heard this year. Such moments seemed out of place.

Led Zeppelin are a symbol of this and probably deserve that position.

At times they did play rock'n'roll as immense and intense as it's possible to get considering the necessary limitations the group occasionally impose upon themselves. But when they lost that discipline and pretended they could be profound and subtle, they were tedious: a true progressive rock group. And the reason progressive rock declined so decisively was because of the musicians' appaulling smugness and dogmatism, their careless determination that they could stretch into areas where their experience and understanding was minimal. Zeppelin were no exception.

But they are one of the few groups of that era and that school of thought who can make some sort of sense in the contemporary scheme of things. Perhaps out of curiousity or desperation, they did blend their base heavy rock with all sorts of vague strains and they also attempted to pushout the borders of heavy metal by exploring the possibilities of repetition and structure.

When Led Zeppelin play rock'n'roll - and 'Trampled Underfoot' is a classic example - I can begin to understand why people call them the greatest. But I can't agree with that statement because when the group lose the discipline, when they indulge themselves, when they naively romanticise and sentimentalise, they are infuriating.

Never have I heard a group so magnificent and so appalling within the space of one set.

During John Paul Jones' flat and uneventful piano part in 'No Quarter', it was sad that they could get away with ineffectual drivel. And yet only the rock'n'roll of Joy Division, Public Image, The Clash and The Raincoats has moved me as much this year as their tumultuous, crushingly compressed version of 'Trampled Underfoot'.

Bringing in such names as The Raincoats is a good way of attempting to put things into perspective, and of defining the distinctions contained in 'the dislocation'.

Led Zeppelin are held in reverential awe even by those who openly despise them. This is ridiculous. It means that the new music, dismissed by the progressive music community as trivial and transient, is not mentioned in the same breath as the group. The thought that Led Zeppelin are somehow 'above' the new music is poisonous, but definitely established.

One of the major benefits of Zeppelin playing Knebworth is that even in their comparative triumph they shatter such illusions. They reduced themselves. It need not be avoided any more, nor is it particularly detrimental, to say that the majority of the masterfully produced but erratic and naive music the group recorded has been surpassed many times over by young groups thrown up by punk.

It is the phenomenon of Zeppelin that should

be held in awe, hardly the music. But, equally, it is the myth and misfortune that should be despisd and pitied, not the music.

Led Zeppelin have made great rock'n'roll. They can fit into what rock'n'roll is about now as well as the Stones or The Who - and you can take that whatever way you want. Certainly they don't deserve to be bracketed anywhere near so-called 'heavy' bands like Judas Priest, Van Halen, Kiss or Rainbow.

I'm considering them in a contemporary per-specitve, finding them not awkward or flatulent at all but in lots of ways exciting. In fact, I'm saying Zeppelin deserve some respect.

Surely the struggle, wearily overcoming the pressures and problems of the last few years, should be admired not snorted at? Are we so intol-erant of groups facing up to the unknown music business obstacles, the loss of ambition, the pres-sures of misplaced idolatry, the expectations, the ageing process?

They come back faced with ridiculously unfair complications, and all we can say is: what took you so long?

There is no reason why Zeppelin should ever speak again; no one has any right to demand activ-ity. One of the bravest moves of the year must be Zeppelin perfoming when the blanket of suspi-cion, cynicism and indeed hate must have been suffocating.

Dissolution

With the successful live reunion of Knebworth behind them, Zeppelin decided to tour again in 1980, prior to considering further recordings. Rather than plunge full-tilt into another of the vast US stadium jaunts of yore, however, they opted for a European tour (the first of any size for seven years), playing a less taxing set (ie, under three hours) in medium-sized indoor venues. The trek opened in Dortmund on June 17, and finished in Berlin on July 7, following just one hiccup when a show in Nuremberg was truncated due to John Bonham being ill.

Another US visit was clearly the next move after this, and an Autumn tour was planned. The band reunited for rehearsals on September 24th and returned to Page's Thames-side house in Windsor for a celebratory party. On September 25th, John Bonham was found dead in bed, having asphixiated while sleeping off a huge vodka bout. Devastated, Page, Plant and Jones cancelled all plans, and early in December made the official announcement to the world that without Bonham, the band could not continue. Led Zeppelin was no more.

Led Zeppelin Uber Alles!

Steve Gett, July 12 1980

Munich's Marineplatz was bustling with shoppers, street salesmen and a variety of side-show acts including ballet dancers and fire-eaters. Contrasted with the discreet bourgeoisie were several denim-clad German youths displaying Led Zeppelin ephemera. Noticing my Zep T-shirt a couple of them approvingly greeted me with: "Led Zeppelin! Led Zeppelin! Ja! Ja!" After a lengthy absence "the boys were back in town" and everyone knew it.

Down in the U-Bahn (the city's underground train system) an array of fans was making its way to the gigantic Olympic Hall for the evening's concert. Meanwhile, several miles away at the Hilton Hotel, other Deutsch devotees were lurking in the lobby hoping to glimpse their idols. Earlier the band had appeared briefly to sign autographs but now were up in their rooms, closely guarded by security as they relaxed prior to the show.

While Zeppelin fever has for the past few weeks enveloped the Continent, not a word has appeared in the English press on what marks the act's first tour for three years.

A number of diehard fans have crossed the Channel in the past fortnight to witness the gigs - but there has been no media coverage whatsoever on Zeppelin's long-awaited return to work. Amazing, when one considers that the band are still by far the most popular outfit in the world.

En route to Munich, encounters with a number of Zep fanatics revealed that the dates have been going extremely well. There seemed to be a feeling of total rejuvenation within the group. The majority of the concerts had sold out and the only minor problem had been the cancellation of the

Nuremberg show due to John Bonham's sheer physical exhaustion.

Munich's Olympic Hall was packed long before the band were due on at 9pm. Souvenir salesmen and the refreshment stands cleaned up during the wait, then shortly before nine kids were anxiously seeking vantage points to watch the gig.

The auditorium is not dissimilar to Wembley, except that there is no seating in the Arena. Consequently fans surged forward to the front huddling together like the proverbial sardines, so that eventually the familiar figure of Harvey Goldsmith emerged to persuade everyone to move back. "This request will be repeated in German," he announced. It wasn't. I suspect it would have been ignored.

Just after a quarter past nine the houselights were switched off, the cue for Munich's Olympic Hall to erupt with more force than a volcano as Zeppelin were greeted with Teutonic fervour. In view of the uncertainty that the band would ever do another concert after Knebworth last year, this was indeed a magical moment.

Fantasy soon turned to reality as the stage illuminated and Jimmy Page hammered out the beginning of "Train Kept A Rollin".

It took some time before Robert fully unleashed, and at the start of the show it was hard to hear him properly, but once under way his vocal performance was tremendous. The second number was "Nobody's Fault But Mine", after which Page himself took the microphone to bid good evening to the crowd and introduce "Black Dog" - incredible but true, Jimmy Page actually speaks on stage!

Indeed it was Jimmy, most of all, who epitomised the new-found enthusiasm of the group. His guitar playing was excellent - rough at times but any errors were covered by moments of inspired genius.

Page dropped his trusty Les Paul in favour of a Strat for "In the Evening" which featured a marvellously serene keyboard passage from John Paul Jones in the slow section. He switched again to his twin-neck Gibson for the softer "Rain Song" and it was here that Plant really came into his element.

The euphoric attitude of the band was communicated with the ensuing song "Hot Dog", and the country and western tune from "In Through The Out Door".

Robert made continual pleas for the fans to spread out and ease the discomfort of those in the front, but like Harvey Goldsmith he was fighting an impossible task. The set had been altered slightly from Knebworth with "No Quarter" and Jimmy's violin bow extravanganze having been dropped.

After "All My love" Robert once again implored everyone in the arena to move back, slipping in his familiar cries of "Push! Push! Push!" - this made an appropriate intro for "Trampled Underfoot". Again Page stole the show with sparkling lead breaks and some wah-wah at the end was possibly the finest guitar of the night.

This was followed by "Since I've Been Lovin' You", a classic in its own right, which anyone who has ever witnessed Zeppelin live will attest is a gem in concert. Here Page

and Plant shared the limelight with tremendous guitar and vocal blues.

"This is the first tour we've done for three years," proclaimed Robert, "and it's certainly been an interesting sketch! And after this - well, who knows?"

Following Plant's brief remarks the band launched headfirst into "Achilles' Last Stand" where Bonzo proved his talents as a sticks man. Next came Jimmy's guitar interlude, based around "White Summer" and "Black Mountain Side". He sat on a chair, alone on stage, but even then wasn't able to stop moving around. To me, this was the only tedious part of the show, which to that juncture had run very smoothly without any lengthy solos.

The whole concert reflected Zeppelin getting back to basics and I think perhaps it might be as well not to include the Page solo spot in order to sustain impetus throughout. Certainly Page has ample opportunity to show his skills during the set and in fact on the preceding number, "Since I've Been Lovin' You", he handled an elongated lead

break. He finished his virtuoso display by leading into "Kashmir". Then came the climax of the set as Zep played their anthem "Stairway to Heaven".

Following the completion of the main set, another drum kit was set up on stage between Robert's mike stand and John Paul Jones' keyboards, which naturally bewildered the audience. Then, after a rendition of "Rock And Roll", Robert introduced Bad Company's Simon Kirke. Together the five musicians delivered an extended version of "Whole Lotta Love". Plant was accompanied by Page on backing vocals (!) and this made a fine ending to the show. When it was over, the band quit the stage to tumultuous applause.

It was one of the most enjoyable gigs I have experienced and certainly the best this year. The group enjoyed themselves as much as the audince.

"Someone once asked me what technicalities I applied to my drumming. I said technicalities, what the hell are you on about? I said this is my technicality and raised my hand in the air and let it fall down hard. Head to drum, that's what it is, just head to drum and the harder the better."

John Bonham - The beat behind Zeppelin Head, heart and drums

by Chris Charlesworth

October 4th, 1980

Bonzo was tough. He played the drums - and life - like a wrecking ball. His technique - if he'll forgive the term - was to emulate nothing less than rolling thunder, pitting his big, brawny physique against anything that the Ludwig drum manufacturers could build to stand up to him. Loudness was the key, the louder the better, and Bonzo's thundering, rumbling bass drum kept Led Zeppelin on a course that took them into a superstar class of their very own.

Everything that Led Zeppelin represented - gigantic spectacle, great wealth, massive musical

power and keeping audiences at a distance - is grossly unfashionable in the current climate of British popular music, but this wasn't always the case.

Time was when extraordinary success throughout the world was something the music press encouraged, especially when the success involved a British band who conquered the world and brought back the spoils like returning soldiers.

From 1969 to 1978, Led Zeppelin did just that. The glitter may have tarnished a little of late, but it once outshone everything that British rock had to offer.

In 1968 Bonham was playing with singer Robert Plant in the Midlands group Band Of Joy, which broke up when Plant was invited by ace guitar virtuoso Jimmy Page to join a new line-up he was hoping to put together in London after the final demise of the Yardbirds.

Pressed to find a drummer for an upcoming Scandinavian tour (on which the group was actually billed as the New Yardbirds), Plant suggested Bonham, who readily obliged. After the Scandinavian tour there were three appearances in England as the New Yardbirds (at Sussex University on October 15, at London's Marquee on October 18 and Liverpool University a day later) before Keith Moon - so rumour has it - suggested the name Led Zeppelin and they set about conquering the world.

Bonham's essential part in all this was the

Left

Jones and Page at rehearsals for

European tour at London

New Victoria Theatre

Above

Page in rare shot with Lake Placid

Blue Stratocaster

Right

The Tour That Time Forgot – Plant and

Page onstage in Brussels. A blistering

series of shows were performed with no

marathon solos

Far Right

Page – Stairway To Heaven

uncanny ability to tumble like a ton of bricks at just the right moment.

Though Zeppelin's studio sound was created by Page, the timing of his rolls - the accuracy of his punches - was an instinct that came from sheer physical strength rather than technique. The boom of the bass and the deep snare, coupled with an eternal solidness that characterises the best of hard rock drumming was all there.

With Page at the controls, this powerful drum machine put down some of the mightiest drum tracks ever recorded.

This deep sound, which came from loose skins, heavy sticks and a brickie's biceps, is as apparent on "Led Zeppelin I" as it was on "In Through The Out Door", their last album.

"Good Times Bad Times", the seminal open-ing number on the first of the band's nine albums, introduced the world to a different kind of rock'n'roll sound and, though the sheer attack came from guitar and vocals, the drums carried the music like a locomotive train. Even on the quieter songs Bonham often managed to cannon in to emphasise the intensity of Plant's lyrics or the scream of Page's guitar.

On "Whole Lotta Love", the song which set the standard for all future heavy metal riffing, Bonham's peculiar talent is best expressed as he punctuates Page's guitar following the free form sonic boom session after the opening verses. As drums and guitar respond, the basic, simple riff re-emerges in a tremendous surge of energy that takes off like no other band.

That same album - Led Zeppelin II - includes

"Moby Dick", Bonham's erstwhile drum solo which he performed at virtually every concert in the group's career. "Dick" gave Bonham a chance to explode and the highlight of the event - which invariably lasted up to twenty minutes - was when he threw the sticks aside and played with his bare hands.

Speed and volume rather than complex timing changes characterised Bonham's solos and if critics accused him of simplicity they missed an obvious point: Bonham drummed for Led Zeppelin not for improvised modern jazz - and the technical perfectionist could no sooner carry Led Zeppelin than you or I.

Bonham's death will almost certainly mean the end of Led Zeppelin.

When Keith Moon died, Pete Townshend used

the opportunity to reshape the Who and burst back with a flurry of activity, but it is doubtful whether the reclusive Jimmy Page will want - or have the motivation and energy - to similarly reshape Led Zeppelin.

The rigidity of their style, the very nature of the band, precludes any shift in direction. This, seems to indicate that the Led Zeppelin juggernaut has finally been laid to rest.

Enormous success and personal tragedy have gone hand in hand throughout Led Zeppelin's roller-coaster of a career. Certainly there have been ugly moments, but I prefer to remember the good times.

Once, when I was reporting on the band from Montreux, I chanced in on a sound check before a performance after bravely eluding the tight security. Sitting alone and unobserved in the balcony I watched in amazement as Led Zeppelin played through the Elvis songbook with more swing than I can ever recall from a heavy rock unit.

John Bonham was an integral part of that unit and, like millions of others who caught Led Zeppelin at their very best, I deeply regret his passing.

Phil Collins

"I can't believe it. John Bonham was one of my all time heroes, and I remember he was one of the first drummers I stood up and clapped for way back in the old Marquee days, before he joined

Zeppelin, when Bonham played in a trio backing the guitarist and singer Tim Rose.

"Of his type of drummer, there was no equal - he was up there with Keith Moon.

"You used to keep hearing all these stories about what a weird bloke he was, but I met him at the Melody Maker Poll Awards party last year and he was charming.

"Things are getting too close to home. When Bolan died, it shook me and a lot of others. We expect these people we grew up with to go on for ever. But they don't, and when it happens, it's a shaker.

"Bonham's death is a loss to music and the tragic end to another little bit of rock 'n' roll history.

Cozy Powell

It's always very difficult to write a piece about someone you like as a professional and a friend, when suddenly they are with you no more.

Bonzo, as he was known to those people who really knew him well, was a real force to be reckoned with. I don't know any one drummer who in his heart of hearts didn't have a soft spot for him.

A notorious hell-raiser at times he may have been; but underneath all that there was a kind and generous man.

First impressions, speaking as a drummer, are always most vivid.

I fondly remember seeing Bonzo for the first time back in 1967 when he was still with Robert Plant's outfit the Band Of Joy in Birmingham.

I was completely staggered by the sheer power and dynamics of his playing, always keeping the beat fairly simple, but occasionally he would let fly with a devasting power around the kit, only to return once more to the business of what the business of drumming is really all about - laying it down and no messing.

As an old friend I'd bump into John Bonham now and again in all sorts of unlikely and out-of-the-way places

Whether it be in a hotel suite in Los Angeles or rehearsal studios anywhere in the world, he would always manage to find the time for a chat and a drink to discuss old times.

As a fellow rock'n'roll drummer he was, certainly in my book, number one, and he always will be.

His unique sound and style of playing will never be forgotten. I have nothing but the utmost respect for John.

Led Zeppelin and the music business to whom he has given so much pleasure will miss himmore than dearly.

To his wife Pat and their two children - my deepest sympathy.

B.P. Fallon, former Led Zeppelin publicist and a close friend

John Bonham is dead. God knows why The Mainman chose him.

It's all a scramble in my mind. Trying to condense in cold print emotions of love and craziness and magic.

Magic? There's so much bullshit in the Fleet Street rags about Led Zeppelin's bad karma. Excuse me while I puke. Zeppo have given more pleasure to more millions than possibly any other band in the world. And with the pleasure has come

John Bonham was a unique drummer admired by fan and respected by fellow musicians. His trademark solo "Moby Dick" would sometimes last over thirty minutes, combining thunderous cascades with subtle light and shade nuances. He would often disregard his drumsticks and play with his bare hands until they bled – a true innovator!

Top

A picture of sartorial elegance.

Jimmy Page sports designer

baggy suit

Below

Jones and Page share a joke at

rehearsals. Does anybody

remember laughter?

Far right

"Eye thank Yew'

The end of an era

the pain. God knows why....

Fragments of memories are burning through my mind.

Like being at Bonzo's house and his son Jason playing a James Brown record on the jukebox and playing along to it brilliantly on the small drumkit his father had bought him. If James Brown had been there he would have been as proud and as smiling as Jason's dad.

Like being in a Lear Jet with Zeppelin when Bonzo took it into his head to pilot this small executive rocket. Bits of chicken legs and bottles of champagne swizzing around the tiny cabin as Bonzo looped the loop;

it was so exhilaratingly terrifying that all we could do was laugh and hang on to our seats, literally.

Like one night at the Continental Hyatt House in LA when some craziness convinced me to get Bonzo, Jonesy, Robert, Jimmy and Roy Harper to dress up in drag. Bonzo, bearded and wearing a silver turban with eyes painted like a reject hooker, was particularly hilarious. Stevie Wonder couldn't figure why all the Atlantic big nobs were freaking out.

Fled in horror

Ahmet Ertegun, who was throwing the party, took one look at the biggest group Atlantic had ever had and hastily fled, horror masking his face. As he hurried nervously into his limo several stories below, Ahmet glanced up at the balcony way above to see four tarts who had conquered America's females wearing lipstick and eye makeup and feather boas and blowing kisses in his direction.

Like taking Zeppo down to The Roxy in '77 to see The Damned. Both bands fell in love with each other. I took Rat Scabies to a Zep rehearsal and Bonzo had just been voted number one drummer in the MM Poll. Rat had been voted number ten. "If I'd had as much sulphate as you," Bonzo teased the Damned drummer, "it'd probably be me at tenth place."

Rat:"I stole a lot of Bonzo's playing and

speeded it up." Last Friday, the Damned appeared in Huddersfield and played Zep's "Rock And Roll", and during Rat's solo in "Neat, Neat, Neat"he played it hand-style,Bonzo style.

Rat on Bonzo's death: "There's nothing worse when someone like Bonzo dies. You don't know what to say. Everyone should be grateful to him for revolutionising a whole attitude to playing."

Dave Edmunds: "He was a nice guy. It doesn't need me to say he was a great drummer. To remain

that unaffected by their success - I'd be well chuffed."

Bob Geldof: "He deserved his place as one of the great British drummers. Without him Led Zeppelin wouldn't have had the initial success they had so amazingly quickly. His drumming was as noticeable as Page's guitar playing. You noticed the drumming. You'd go 'Jesus' at the drumming. It's just sad."

When Wings played Birmingham last autumn Bonzo came backstage to say hi to Paul and Linda. They were delighted to see him. When I spoke to Paul the other day he was lost for words, and yet in one sentence he summed John Bonham up: "He was one of the greats."

God bless you, Bonzo.

Concert Analysis

1968

After an intense rehearsal period, the band's first shows were played in Scandinavia in September 1968. These initial performances are believed to have been of 35 - 45 minutes duration and included the following numbers:

Train Kept A Rollin'
I Can't Quit You
Dazed and Confused
You Shook Me
How Many More Times

Blues standards such as Otis Rush's "I Gotta Move" are also known to have been played (Stockholm 20 Sept 68).

1969

For the first US tour (commencing 26 Dec 68) the set had been expanded to encompass much of the material from the first album. Set length would vary according to circumstances and would range from 60 minutes for a Festival appearance (Dallas Pop Festival 31 Aug 69) to 140 minutes for those concerts where the group would play two sets per evening (San Francisco 27 Apr 69). At the Boston Tea Party (28 Jan 69) the band are reported to have played for four and a half hours.

Songs featured during 1969 were:

Train Kept A Rollin'
I Can't Quit You
Dazed and Confused
As Long As I Have You
White Summer

Pat's Delight
Killing Floor/Lemon Song
You Shook Me
Babe I'm Gonna Leave You
How Many More Times

Encore:
Communication Breakdown

"As Long As I Have You" (a Garnett Mimms blues standard) and "How Many More Times" were frequently expanded to allow improvisation and numerous blues references were included in the medleys including "Fresh Garbage", "Shake", "Hush Little Baby", "The Hunter", "Smokestack Lightning", "Cat's Squirrel", "Cadillac", "I'm A Man" and "For What Its Worth". Page occasionally referred back to his Yardbirds past by playing "Over Under Sideways Down" and "For Your Love" (San Francisco 10 Jan 69).

"Whole Lotta Love" was premiered at Winterland, San Francisco on 26 Apr 69 but was not played frequently until the following year.

At the Lyceum, London concert (12 Oct 69), "Heartbreaker" and "What Is And What Should Never Be" were introduced into the set and by November "Moby Dick" replaced "Pat's Delight" as John Bonham's showcase.

1970

The group started 1970 with a new opening number "We're Gonna Groove" (a Ben E King cover).

We're Gonna Groove
I Can't Quit You
Dazed and Confused

Heartbreaker
Bring It On Home
White Summer/Black Mountain Side
Since I've Been Loving You
Thank You
What Is And What Should Never Be
Moby Dick
How Many More Times

Encores:
Whole Lotta Love
Communication Breakdown

John Paul Jones introduced a keyboard solo to the set leading into "Thank You" and "How Many More Times" was expanded further to feature even more blues standards.

Rock and roll classics were used for extra encores wherever required. These included "Johnny B. Goode", "Great Balls Of Fire", "Long Tall Sally", "Something Else", "C'mon Everybody" and "Blueberry Hill".

The Bath Festival (28 Jun 70) saw "Immigrant Song" replace "We're Gonna Groove" as the opening number, also "That's The Way" was introduced to the set (initially called "The Boy Next Door").

From the sixth US tour in Aug 1970, the "Bron-Y-Aur" instrumental was played and "How Many More Times" was removed to allow "Whole Lotta Love" to be expanded as the main vehicle for improvisation.

1971

The concerts played in 1971 were frequently 2 - 3 hours long and featured:

Immigrant Song
Heartbreaker
Since I've Been Loving You
Black Dog
Stairway to Heaven
Celebration Day
Dazed and Confused
Going to California
That's The Way
What Is And What Should Never Be
Moby Dick
Whole Lotta Love

Encores:
Communication Breakdown
Thank You
Rock And Roll

"Stairway to Heaven" was premiered at Belfast on 5 Mar 71. "Four Sticks" and "Gallows Pole" were played in Copenhagen on 3 May 71 but were apparently never played again! "Misty Mountain Hop" was also played at this concert, but would not feature regularly in the set for another year and a half.

The first Japanese tour introduced the live debut's of "Bron-Y-Aur Stomp" and "Tangerine". "Friends" was played at Osaka on 29 Sep 71 but seemingly not played again.

"Dancing Days" was previewed at the Electric Magic concerts at Wembley, London in Nov 71.

1972

The Australian and US tours continued with a similar set to 1971. However, for the second Japanese tour in October, the set changed to reflect material from the "Houses Of The Holy" album.

Rock And Roll
Over The Hills And Far Away
Black Dog
Misty Mountain Hop
Since I've Been Loving You

Dancing Days
Bron-Y-Aur Stomp
The Song Remains The Same
The Rain Song
Dazed and Confused
Stairway to Heaven
Whole Lotta Love

Encores:
Immigrant Song
Heartbreaker
Thank You
Communication Breakdown

Unusual performances in 1972 included "Let's Dance/Louie Louie" and "Money" at Seattle 19 Jun 72 and "Stand By Me" at Osaka 9 Oct 72. The "Whole Lotta Love" medley was by now, fre-

quently including "Everybody Needs Somebody", "Let That Boy Boogie", "Hello Mary Lou", "Let's Have A Party", "I Can't Quit You" and "Going Down Slow" amongst many others.

1973

The UK and Europe tour featured a similar set to the 1972 concerts. However, for the US tour in May 1973, the set had evolved into:

Rock And Roll
Celebration Day
Black Dog
Over The Hills And Far Away
Misty Mountain Hop
Since I've Been Loving You

No Quarter
The Song Remains The Same
The Rain song
Dazed and Confused
Stairway to Heaven
Moby Dick
Heartbreaker
Whole Lotta Love

Encores:
The Ocean
Communication Breakdown

The introduction of "No Quarter" allowed John Paul Jones the opportunity for a keyboard solo again, John Bonham's solo "Moby Dick" was reintroduced and "Dazed and Confused" had developed into a 30 minute plus epic, featuring Page's pyrotechnic "violin bow" guitar solos. "Dancing Days" reappeared as a very rare third encore. It is from the July concerts at Madison Square Gardens, New York, that the groups only official live album "The Song Remains The Same" originates.

1975

After a lengthy period of inactivity the band returns to live action with the following set, featuring tracks from "Physical Graffiti":

Rock And Roll
Sick Again
Over The Hills And Far Away
In My Time Of Dying
The Song Remains The Same
The Rain Song
Kashmir
No Quarter
Trampled Underfoot
Moby Dick
Dazed and Confused
Stairway to Heaven

Encores:
Whole Lotta Love/The Crunge/Black Dog
Heartbreaker
Communication Breakdown
The Initial shows of the tour also featured "When The Levee Breaks" and "The Wanton Song" but these numbers were soon removed.

"How Many More Times" was played instead of "Dazed and Confused" on the initial US dates, due to Page's sprained finger.

The UK dates at Earls Court, London in May 75 also featured an acoustic set comprised of "Tangerine", "Going To California", "That's The Way" and "Bron-Y-Aur Stomp".

1977

The 1977 US tour set consistently featured performances of more than 3 hours and included the following songs:
The Song Remains The Same
Sick Again
Nobody's Fault But Mine
In My Time Of Dying
Since I've Been Loving You
No Quarter
Ten Years Gone
Battle Of Evermore
Going To California
Bron-Y-Aur Stomp
White Summer
Kashmir
Trampled Underfoot
Moby Dick
Page Solo
Achilles Last Stand
Stairway to Heaven
Encore:
Whole Lotta Love/Rock And Roll

"No Quarter" was now extended to 30 minutes duration to allow Jones more scope for improvisation. John Bonham solo's (sometimes now referred

to as "Over The Top") was also now extended and Page's solo often included "The Star Spangled Banner". "Heartbreaker" was occasionally played as the tour progressed and "Black Dog", "Communication Breakdown" and Jerry Lee Lewis's "It'll Be Me" were infrequently featured as an extra encore.

1979

The Knebworth Festivals and the Copenhagen "warm-up" shows featured new material from the forthcoming "In Through The Out Door" album and songs reintroduced from the past repertoire.

The Song Remains The Same
Celebration Day
Black Dog
Nobody's Fault But Mine
Over The Hills And Far Away
Misty Mountain Hop
Since I've Been Loving You
No Quarter
Ten Years Gone
Hot Dog
The Rain Song
White Summer
Kashmir

Trampled Underfoot
Sick Again
Achilles Last Stand
Page Solo
In The Evening
Stairway to Heaven

Encores:
Rock And Roll
Whole Lotta Love
"Heartbreaker" was played as an additional encore at Knebworth on 4 Aug 79 as was "Communication Breakdown" on 11 Aug 79.

The most notable absence from the set was John Bonham's solo. This heralded the beginning of a sleeker, less excessive Led Zeppelin.

1980

The set had now been trimmed down to two hours duration, concentrating on songs rather than solos:

Train Kept A Rollin'
Nobody's Fault But Mine

Black Dog
In The Evening
The Rain Song
Hot Dog
All My Love
Trampled Underfoot
Since I've Been Loving You
Achilles Last Stand
White Summer
Kashmir
Stairway to Heaven

Encore:
Rock And Roll

"Train Kept A Rollin'" was reintroduced as a surprise opening number - the band had not played this live since 1969!
  "Whole Lotta Love", "Heartbreaker" and "Communication Breakdown" were alternated as a second encore. "Money" was played at Frankfurt on 30 Jun 80. The European tour ended in Berlin on 7 Jul 80.
  The Band were in preparation for a major US tour when the tragic death of John Bonham occurred at Jimmy Page's Mill House in Windsor on 25 Sep 80.

Concert Log

First Scandinavian tour

14-9-68   Copenhagen, Denmark
          (billed as the 'New Yardbirds')
15-9-69   Copenhagen, Denmark
17-9-69   Malmo, Sweden*
18-9-68   Gothenburg, Sweden*
20-9-68   Stockholm, Sweden
21-9-68   Stockholm, Sweden
22-9-68   Bergen, Norway*
23-9-68   Oslo, Norway
24-9-68   Oslo, Norway

First UK tour

15-10-68 Surrey University
18-10-68 London - Marquee
19-10-68 Liverpool University
9-11-68   London - Roundhouse (1st show billed as
'Led Zeppelin' - Plant marries on same day)
16-11-68 Manchester - College of Science and
          Technology
23-11-68 Sheffield University
10-12-68 London - Marquee
16-12-68 Bath - Pavillion
19-12-68 Exeter - City Hall
20-12-68 London - Fishmongers Hall,
          Wood Green

First US tour

26-12-68 Denver - Coliseum
27-12-68 Seattle - Centre Arena
30-12-68 Spokane - Gonzaga Gym
31-12-68 Portland

2-1-69   Los Angeles - Whiskey A Go Go
3-1-69   Los Angeles - Whiskey A Go Go
4-1-69   Los Angeles - Whiskey A Go Go
5-1-69   Los Angeles - Whiskey A Go Go
9-1-69   San Francisco - Fillmore West
10-1-69 San Francisco - Fillmore West
11-1-69 San Francisco - Fillmore West
13-1-69 San Diego - Fox Theatre
14-1-69 Fort Worth
15-1-69 Houston
16-1-69 New Orleans
17-1-69 Detroit - Grande Ballroom
18-1-69 Detroit - Grande Ballroom
21-1-69 Miami - Image Club
22-1-69 Atlanta
24-1-69 Baltimore
25-1-69 Pittsburg
26-1-69 Cleveland
28-1-69 Boston - Boston Tea Party
29-1-69 Philadelphia
31-1-69 New York - Fillmore East
         (support to Iron Butterfly)
1-2-69   New York - Fillmore East
2-2-69   Toronto, Canada - Rockpile
7-2-69   Chicago - Kinetic Playground
8-2-69   Chicago - Kinetic Playground

Second UK tour

1-3-69   London - Fishmongers Hall
3-3-69   Plymouth
5-3-69   Cardiff
7-3-69   Hornsey Wood - Bluesville 69 Club
10-3-69 Edmonton - Cooks Ferry Inn
12-3-69 Leicester

Second Scandinavian tour

13-3-69 Copenhagen, Denmark - Gladsaxe
         Teen Club (Evening)
13-3-69 Copenhagen, Denmark -
         (Danish TV - Afternoon)
14-3-69 Stockholm, Sweden - Koncerthaus
15-3-69 Stockholm, Sweden - Koncerthaus
16-3-69 Oslo, Norway
17-3-69 Oslo, Norway
18-3-69 Copenhagen, Denmark

Second UK tour continues

21-3-69 London - How Late It Is (TV show)
22-3-69 Birmingham - Mothers Club
24-3-69 Edmonton - Cooks Ferry Inn
25-3-69 Staines - Supershow (recording)
28-3-69 London - Marquee
30-3-69 Southall - Farx Club
1-4-69   Hamstead - Klooks Kleek
5-4-69   London - Roundhouse
8-4-69   Welwyn Garden City - Cherry Tree
12-4-69 Tolworth - Toby Jug
14-4-69 Stoke on Trent
17-4-69 Sunderland

Second US tour

18-4-69	New York, University Jazz Festival
24-4-69	San Francisco - Fillmore West
25-4-69	San Francisco - Winterland Ballroom
26-4-69	San Francisco - Winterland Ballroom
27-4-69	San Francisco - Fillmore West
29-4-69	Los Angeles - Whiskey A Go Go
30-4-69	Los Angeles - Whiskey A Go Go
1-5-69	Irvine - Crawford Hall
2-5-69	Passadena - Rose Palace
3-5-69	Passadena - Rose Palace
4-5-69	Santa Monica
5-5-69	Santa Monica
9-5-69	Portland
10-5-69	Vancouver
11-5-69	Seattle - Aquatheatre
13-5-69	Honolulu - International Centre
16-5-69	Detroit - Grande Ballroom
17-5-69	Athens - Ohio University
18-5-69	Minneapolis - Guthrie Memorial Theatre
19-5-69	Boston - Boston Gardens
21-5-69	Syracuse
22-5-69	Philadelphia
23-5-69	Chicago - Kinetic Playground
24-5-69	Chicago - Kinetic Playground
25-5-69	Columbia - Merriweather Post Pavillion
26-5-69	Pittsburg
27-5-69	Cleveland
28-5-69	Boston - Boston Tea Party
29-5-69	Boston - Boston Tea Party
30-5-69	New York - Fillmore East
31-5-69	New York - Fillmore East

Third UK tour

8-6-69	Newcastle - City Hall
13-6-69	Birmingham - Town Hall
15-6-69	Manchester - Free Trade Hall
20-6-69	Newcastle - City Hall
21-6-69	Bristol - Colston Hall
25-6-69	Paris, France - Antenne Culturelle (French TV Recording)
26-6-69	Portsmouth - Guildhall
27-6-69	London - Playhouse Theatre (BBC recording)
28-6-69	Bath - Blues Festival (Attendance - 12,000)
29-6-69	London - Royal Albert Hall (2 shows)

Third US tour

5-7-69	Atlanta - Atlanta Pop Festival
6-7-69	Newport - Newport Pop Festival
8-7-69	Miami
9-7-69	Tampa
10-7-69	Jacksonville
11-7-69	Baltimore - Laurel Pop Festival
12-7-69	Philadelphia - Jazz Festival
13-7-69	New York - Singer Bowl
15-7-69	Rochester, NY
16-7-69	Cleveland
17-7-69	Cincinnati
18-7-69	Chicago - Kinetic Playground
19-7-69	Chicago - Kinetic Playground
20-7-69	Detroit
21-7-69	New York - Central park
25-7-69	Milwaukee - West Allis
26-7-69	St. Paul
29-7-69	Seattle - Woodinville Festival
29-7-69	Vancouver, Canada
30-7-69	Portland
31-7-69	Eugene
1-8-69	Santa Barbara
2-8-69	Los Angeles - Coliseum
3-8-69	Houston - Music Hall
4-8-69	Dallas - Coliseum
6-8-69	Sacramento - Memorial Auditorium
7-8-69	Berkeley - Community Theatre
8-8-69	San Bernardino - Swing Auditorium
9-8-69	Anaheim - Convention Centre
10-8-69	San Diego - Sports Arena
11-8-69	San Francisco - Fillmore West
13-8-69	New Haven
14-8-69	Springfield
15-8-69	Boston
16-8-69	Boston
17-8-69	Wallingford - Oakdale Theatre
18-8-69	Toronto, Canada - Rockpile (2 shows) "Mighty Monday"
19-8-69	Detroit
20-8-69	Indianapolis
21-8-69	St Louis
22-8-69	Denver
24-8-69	Jacksonville - Veterans Memorial Coliseum
25-8-69	Salt Lake City
27-8-69	Los Angeles - Coliseum
28-8-69	San Diego
29-8-69	Pheonix
30-8-69	New York - Singer Bowl
31-8-69	Dallas - Texas International Pop Festival

10-10-69	Paris-Olympia Theatre
12-10-69	London - Lyceum Ballroom (Triumphant UK return)

Fourth US tour

17-10-69	New York - Carnegie Hall (Two Shows)
18-10-69	Detroit - Olympia Stadium
19-10-69	Chicago - Kinetic Playground
20-10-69	Cleveland - Music Hall
21-10-69	Philadelphia - Electric Factory
23-10-69	St.Louis
26-10-69	Boston - Boston Gardens
28-10-69	Anaheim - Convention Centre
29-10-69	Seattle
30-10-69	Buffalo - Kleinhans Music Hall
31-10-69	Providence
1-11-69	Syracuse - War Memorial Auditorium
2-11-69	Toronto, Canada - O'Keefe Centre (2 shows - Edward Bear supports)
4-11-69	Kitchener, Canada - Memorial Auditorium
5-11-69	Kansas City - Memorial Hall
6-11-69	San Francisco - Winterland
7-11-69	San Francisco - Winterland
8-11-69	San Francisco - Winterland

Fourth UK tour

7-1-70	Birmingham - Town Hall
8-1-70	Bristol - Colston Hall
9-1-70	London - Royal Albert Hall (Filmed for unbroadcast TV documentary)
13-1-70	Portsmouth - Guild Hall
15-1-70	Newcastle - City Hall
16-1-70	Sheffield - City Hall
24-1-70	Leeds - Town Hall
7-2-70	Edinburgh - Usher Hall (cancelled due to Plant's road accident)

Third Scandinvian tour

23-2-70   Helsinki, Finland
25-2-70   Gottenburg, Sweden
26 2 70   Stockholm, Sweden
27-2-70   Amsterdam, Holland
28-2-70   Copenhagen, Denmark - K.B. Hallen
          (billed as 'The Nobs')

First European tour

2-3-70   Brussels, Belgium
3-3-70   Cologne, Germany
4-3-70   Hanover, Germany
5-3-70   Frankfurt, Germany
6-3-70   Nuremburg, Germany
7-3-70   Geneva, Switzerland -
          Victoria Concert Hall
8-3-70   Munich, Germany - Cirkus Kroner
9-3-70   Vienna, Austria - Koncerthalle
10-3-70   Frankfurt, Germany (cancelled)
11-3-70   Dusseldorf, Germany
12-3-70   Hamburg, Germany - Musikhalle
14-3-70   Montreux, Switzerland - Jazz Festival

Fifth US tour

21-3-70   Vancouver, Canada - PNE Coliseum
22-3-70   Seattle - Centre Arena
23-3-70   Portland - Memorial Coliseum
25-3-70   Denver - Coliseum
26-3-70   San Diego - Sports Arena
27-3-70   Los Angeles - Forum
28-3-70   Dallas - Memorial Auditorium
29-3-70   Houston - Hofheinz Pavilion
30-3-70   New York - Long Island
31-3-70   Toronto, Canada
1-4-70   Boston - Boston Gardens
2-4-70   Detroit - Cobo Hall
3-4-70   Pittsburg
4-4-70   Philadelphia - Spectrum
5-4-70   Baltimore - Civic Centre
6-4-70   Memphis - Ellis Auditorium
7-4-70   Raleigh - Dorten Auditorium
8-4-70   Atlanta - Municipal Auditorium
9-4-70   Tampa - Curtis Nixon Hall
11-4-70   St Louis - Missouri Arena
12-4-70   Chicago - Chicago Amphitheatre
13-4-70   Montreal, Canada
14-4-70   Ottowa, Canada - Civic Centre
15-4-70   Winnipeg, Canada

17-4-70   Salt Lake City
18-4-70   Pheonix - Arizona Coliseum
19-4-70   Las Vegas - Convention Centre
          (cancelled due to Plant's voice)

European Interlude

22-6-70   Reykjavik, Iceland
28-6-70   Bath - Festival (Attendance 150,000)
9-7-70   Cologne, Germany - Sportshalle
10-7-70   Essen, Germany
11-7-70   Frankfurt, Germany - Festhalle
12-7-70   Berlin-Deutschlandhalle

Sixth US tour

5-8-70   Cincinatti (cancelled)
6-8-70   Detroit (cancelled)
7-8-70   Cleveland (cancelled)
8-8-70   Pittsburg (cancelled)
9-8-70   Boston (cancelled)
10-8-70   Hampton - Coliseum
11-8-70   Charlotte
12-8-70   Jacksonville
13-8-70   Tallahassee
14-8-70   Atlanta
15-8-70   New Haven - Yale
16-8-70   Birmingham
17-8-70   Memphis
18-8-70   New Orleans
19-8-70   San Antonio
20-8-70   Fort Worth
21-8-70   Tulsa
22-8-70   Albquerque
24-8-70   St Louis
25-8-70   Chicago
26-8-70   Chicago
27-8-70   Milwaukee
28-8-70   St Paul
29-8-70   Minneapolis
31-8-70   Portland
1-9-70   Seattle - Centre Coliseum
2-9-70   Oakland - Coliseum
3-9-70   San Diego - Sports Arena
4-9-70   Los Angeles - Forum
          "Bluebery Hill" show
5-9-70   Honolulu
6-9-70   Honolulu
9-9-70   Boston - Boston Gardens
14-9-70   Rochester
15-9-70   New Haven
17-9-70   Philadelphia - Spectrum
19-9-70   New York City - Madison Square Garden
          (2 shows)

Fifth UK tour 'Return To The Clubs'

5-3-71   Belfast - Ulster Hall
6-3-71   Dublin - Boxing Stadium (Phil Carson
          Jams on encore)
9-3-71   Leeds - Leeds University
10-3-71   Canterbury - University
11-3-71   Southampton - University
13-3-71   Bath - Pavillion
14-3-71   Stoke, The Place, Hanley
16-3-71   Liverpool (cancelled - due to Plant's voice)
18-3-71   Newcastle, Mayfair
19-3-71   Manchester - University
20-3-71   Birmingham - Stepmothers
21-3-71   Nottingham - Boat Club
23-3-71   London - Marquee
24-3-71   Sutton Coldfield Belfry
25-3-71   London - Paris Theatre (BBC recording)
10-5-71   Liverpool University (rescheduled)

Second European tour

3-5-71   Copenhagen, Denmark - K.B.Hallen
6-6-7   Stockholm, Sweden
8-6-71   Oslo, Norway
9-6-71   Amsterdam, Holland
10-6-71   Rotterdam, Holland
11-6-71   Brussels, Belgium
12-6-71   Bonn, Germany
13-6-71   Dortmund, Germany
15-6-71   Bremen, Germany
16-6-71   Hanover, Germany
17-6-71   Berlin, Germany
18-6-71   Hamburg, Germany
19-6-71   Hamburg, Germany
20-6-71   Essen, Germany
22-6-71   Cologne, Germany
23-6-71   Frankfurt, Germany
24-6-71   Nuremburg, Germany
25-6-71   Vienna, Austria

26-6-71   Munich, Germany
28-6-71   Zurich, Switzerland
2-7-71   Torino, Italy
4-7-71   Rome, Italy
5-7-71   Milan, Italy - Viorelli Stadium
           (show aborted due to crowd riot)

Warm-up shows

7-8-71   Montreux, Switzerland - Casino
8-8-71   Montreux, Switzerland - Casino

Seventh US tour

19-8-71   Vancouver, Canada
20-8-71   Seattle
21-8-71   Los Angeles - Forum
22-8-71   Los Angeles - Forum
23-8-71   Fort Worth
24-8-71   Dallas - Memorial auditorium
25-8-71   Houston
26-8-71   San Antonio
27-8-71   Oklahoma
28-7-71   St Louis
29-8-71   New Orleans - Municipal Auditorium
31-8-71   Orlando - Civic Auditorium
1-9-71   Miami
2-9-71   Pittsburg
3-9-71   New York City - Madison Square Garden
4-9-71   Toronto, Canada - Maple Leaf Gardens
5-9-71   Chicago
7-9-71   Boston - Boston Gardens
9-9-71   Hampton - Hampton Beach
10-9-71   Syracuse
11-9-71   Rochester - Memorial Auditorium
13-9-71   Berkeley - Community Centre
14-9-71   Berkeley - Community Centre
16-9-71   Honolulu
17-9-71   Honolulu

First Japanese tour

23-9-71   Tokyo - Budokan Hall
24-9-71   Tokyo - Budokan Hall
27-9-71   Hiroshima - Municipal Gymnasium
28-9-71   Osaka - Festival Hall
29-9-71   Osaka - Festival Hall

Sixth UK tour

11-11-71 Newcastle - City Hall
12-11-71 Sunderland - Locarno

13-11-71 Dundee - Caird Hall
16-11-71 Ipswich - St Matthews Baths
17-11-71 Birmingham - Kinetic Circus
18-11-71 Sheffield - University
20-11-71 London - Empire Pool "Electric Magic"
21-11-71 London - Empire Pool (Ticket price 75p)
23-11-71 Preston Town Hall
24-11-71 Manchester - Free Trade Hall
25-11-71 Leicester - University
29-11-71 Liverpool - Empire
30-11-71 Manchester - Kings Hall, Belle Vue
2-12-71 Bournemouth - Royal Ballroom "Starkers"
15-12-71 Salisbury - City Hall

Australia/New Zealand tour

16-2-72 Perth - Subiaco Oval
19-2-72 Adelaide - Memorial Drive
          (delayed 1 day - rain)
20-2-72 Melbourne - Kooyong Tennis Courts
24-2-72 Auckland - Western Spring Stadium
27-2-72 Sydney - Showground
29-2-72 Brisbane - Festival Hall

Warm-up shows

5-5-72   Wigan*
6-5-72   Wigan*
7-5-72   Wigan*
27-5-72   Amsterdam, Holland
2-6-72   Brussels, Belgium - Vorst National

Eighth US tour

6-6-72   Detroit - Cobo Hall
7-6-72   Montreal, Canada - Forum
8-6-72   Boston - Boston Gardens
9-6-72   Charlotte - Memorial Coliseum
10-6-72   Buffalo - Memorial Auditorium
11-6-72   Baltimore - Civic Centre
13-6-72   Philadelphia - Spectrum
14-6-72   New York - Nassau Coliseum
15-6-72   New York - Nassau Coliseum

17-6-72   Portland – Memorial Coliseum
18-6-72   Seattle Coliseum
19-6-72   Seattle Coliseum
21-6-72   Denver - Coliseum
22-6-72   San Bernardino - Swing Auditorium
23-6-72   San Diego - Sports Arena
24-6-72   Berkeley - Community Centre
25-6-72   Los Angeles - Forum
27-6-72   Long Beach - Arena
28-6-72   Tuscon - Community Centre (Band
           return to UK on 30/6/72. Further often
           quoted US dates did not exist)

Second Japanese tour

2-10-72 Tokyo - Budokan Hall
3-10-72 Tokyo - Budokan Hall
4-10-72 Osaka - Festival Hall
5-10-72 Nagoya - Kokaido
8-10-72 Osaka - Festival Hall
9-10-72 Osaka - Festival Hall
10-10-72 Kyoto - Kaikan Hall

Return to Montreux

27-10-72 Montreux, Switzerland - Casino
28-10-72 Montreux, Switzerland - Casino

Seventh UK tour

30-11-72 Newcastle - City Hall
1-12-72 Newcastle - City Hall
3-12-72 Glasgow - Greens Playhouse
4-12-72 Glasgow - Greens Playhouse
7-12-72 Manchester - Hardrock
8-12-72 Manchester - Hardrock
11-12-72 Cardiff - Capitol Theatre
12-12-72 Cardiff - Capitol Theatre
16-12-72 Birmingham Odeon
17-12-72 Birmingham Odeon
20-12-72 Brighton - Dome
22-12-72 London - Alexandra Palace
23-12-72 London - Alexandra Palace

2-1-73

Sheffield - City Hall
3-1-73   Preston - Guildhall (cancelled)
4-1-73   Bradford - St Georges Hall
          (cancelled - Plant has flu)
7-1-73   Oxford - New Theatre
14-1-73   Liverpool - Empire
15-1-73   Stoke - Trentham Gardens
16-1-73   Aberystwyth - Kings Hall
18-1-73   Bradford - St Georges Hall (rescheduled)
20-1-73   Southampton - University
          (recorded professionally)
21-1-73   Southampton - Gaumont
25-1-73   Aberdeen - Music Hall
27-1-73   Dundee - Caird Hall
28-1-73   Edinburgh - Kings Theatre
30-1-73   Preston - Guild Hall (rescheduled)

Third European tour

3-3-73   Copenhagen, Denmark
4-3-73   Gothenburg, Sweden
6-3-73   Stockholm, Sweden - Tennishallen
7-3-73   Stockholm, Sweden - Tennishallen
10-3-73   Oslo, Sweden
11-3-73   Rotterdam, Holland
12-3-73   Brussels, Belgium
13-3-73   Frankfurt, Germany
14-3-73   Nuremburg, Germany - Messenhalle
16-3-73   Vienna, Austria - Konserthaus
17-3-73   Munich, Germany - Olympiahalle
19-3-73   Berlin, Germany - Deutschlandhalle
21-3-73   Hamburg, Germany - Musichalle
22-3-73   Essen, Germany - Grughalle
23-3-73   Cologne, Germany
24-3-73   Offenburg, Germany
26-3-73   Lyon, France
27-3-73   Nancy, France
29-3-73   Marseilles, France (cancelled)
31-3-73   Lille, France (cancelled)
1-4-73   Paris, France - Palais des Sport
2-4-73   Paris, France - Palais des Sport

Ninth US tour

4-5-73   Atlanta - Braves Stadium
5-5-73   Tampa - Tampa Stadium
          (Attendance 56,800 - record breaking!)
6-5-73   St Petersburg - Bayfront Civic Auditorium
7-5-73   Jacksonville - the Coliseum
9-5-73   Tuscaloosa - University of Alabama
11-5-73   St Louis - Keil Auditorium
13-5-73   Mobile - Municipal Auditorium
14-5-73   New Orleans - Municipal Auditorium
16-5-73   Houston - Hofheinz Pavilion

18-5-73   Dallas - Memorial Auditorium
19-5-73   Fort Worth - Convention Centre
22-5-73   San Antonio - Municipal Auditorium
23-5-73   Albuquerque - University of New Mexico
25-5-73   Denver - Coliseum
26-5-73   Salt Lake City - Salt Palace
28-5-73   San Diego - Sports Arena
30-5-73   Los Angeles - Forum
          (cancelled - Page sprained finger)
31-5-73   Los Angeles - Forum
2-6-73   San Francisco - Kezar Stadium
3-6-73   Los Angeles - Forum (rescheduled date)
6-7-73   Chicago - Chicago Stadium
7-7-73   Chicago - Chicago Stadium
8-7-73   Indianapolis - Market Square Arena
9-7-73   St Paul - Civic Centre
10-7-73   Milwaukee - Arena
12-7-73   Detroit - Cobo Hall
13-7-73   Detroit - Cobo Hall
15-7-73   Buffalo - War Memorial Auditorium
17-7-73   Seattle - Centre Coliseum
18-7-73   Vancouver, Canada - Coliseum
19-7-73   Philadelphia - Spectrum
20-7-73   Boston - Boston Gardens
21-7-73   Providence - Civic Centre
23-7-73   Baltimore - Civic Centre (Filming
          commences for 'Song Remains The Same')
24-7-73   Pittsburg - Three Rivers Stadium
27-7-73   New York City - Madison Square Garden
28-7-73   New York City - Madison Square Garden
29-9-73   New York City - Madison Square Garden
          ($203,000 stolen from band's hotel)

Warm-up shows

11-1-75   Rotterdam, Holland
12-1-75   Brussels - Vorst National

Tenth US tour

18-1-75   Minneapolis - Metro Sports Centre
20-1-75   Chicago - Chicago Stadium
21-1-75   Chicago - Chicago Stadium
22-1-75   Chicago - Chicago Stadium
24-1-75   Cleveland - Coliseum

25-1-75   Indianapolis - Market Square Arena
26-1-75   St Louis (cancelled)
29-1-75   Greensboro - Coliseum
31-1-75   Detroit - Olympia Hall
1-2-75   Pittsburgh - Civic Arena
2-2-75   Pittsburgh - Civic Arena
3-2-75   New York City - Madison Square Garden
4-2-75   Long Island - Nassua Colisuem
6-2-75   Montreal, Canada - Forum
7-2-75   New York City - Madison Square Garden
8-2-75   Philadelphia - Spectrum
10-2-75   Landover - Capitol Centre
12-2-75   New York City - Madison Square Garden
13-2-75   Long Island - Nassau Coliseum
14-2-75   Long Island - Nassau Coliseum (Ron
          Wood of Rolling Stones jams on
          'Communication Breakdown')
16-2-75   St Louis
27-2-75   Houston
28-2-75   Baton Rouge - State University
1-3-75   New Orleans - Municipal Auditorium
2-3-75   Bent Harbour - University of Tennessee
3-3-75   Fort Worth - Tarrant Convention Centre
4-3-75   Dallas - Memorial Auditorium
5-3-75   Dallas - Memorial Auditorium
7-3-75   Austin
8-3-75   West Palm Beach - Raceway (cancelled)
10-3-75   San Diego - Sports Arena
11-3-75   Long Beach - Pacific Arena
12-3-75   Long Beach - Pacific Arena
17-3-75   Seattle - Coliseum
19-3-75   Vancouver, Canada - Coliseum
20-3-75   Vancouver, Canada - Coliseum
21-3-75   Seattle - Coliseum
24-3-75   Los Angeles - Forum
25-3-75   Los Angeles - Forum
27-3-75   Los Angeles - Forum

UK return

17-5-75   London - Earls Court
18-5-75   London - Earls Court
23-5-75   London - Earls Court
24-5-75   London - Earls Court
25-5-75   London - Earls Court
23-8-75   Oakland - Oakland Stadium
          (cancelled - US tour cancelled due to
          Plant's road accident in Rhodes)
24-8-75   Oakland - Oakland Stadium (cancelled)
6-9-75   Pasadena - Rose Bowl (cancelled)
10-12-75 St Hellier, Jersey - Behans Club (Plant's
          return to stage)

Eleventh US tour

1-4-77	Dallas - Memorial Auditorium
3-4-77	Oklahoma - The Myriad
6-4-77	Chicago - Chicago Stadium
7-4-77	Chicago - Chicago Stadium
9-4-77	Chicago - Chicago Stadium (show aban doned after 1 hour due to Page's illness)
10-4-77	Chicago - Chicago Stadium
12-4-77	Minneapolis - Sports Arena
13-4-77	St Paul - Memorial Coliseum
15-4-77	St Louis - Blues Arena
17-4-77	Indianapolis - Market Square Arena
19-4-77	Cincinnati - Riverfront Coliseum
20-4-77	Cincinnati - Riverfront Coliseum
23-4-77	Atlanta - The Omni
25-4-77	Louisville - Kentucky Fairgrounds
27-4-77	Cleveland - Richfield Coliseum
28-4-77	Cleveland - Richfield Coliseum
30-4-77	Pontiac - Silverdome (record breaking attendance record of 76,229)
18-5-77	Birmingham - Jefferson Coliseum
19-5-77	Baton Rouge - State University
21-5-77	Houston - The Summit
22-5-77	Fort Worth - Convention Centre (Bad Co's Mick Ralphs jams on 'It'll Be Me')
25-5-77	Landover - Capitol Centre
26-5-77	Landover - Capitol Centre
28-5-77	Landover - Capitol Centre
30-5-77	Landover - Capitol Centre
31-5-77	Greensboro - Coliseum
3-6-77	Tampa - Tampa Stadium (show abadoned after 20 mins due to rain)
7-6-77	New York City - Madison Square Garden
8-6-77	New York City - Madison Square Garden
10-6-77	New York City - Madison Square Garden
11-6-77	New York City - Madison Square Garden
13-6-77	New York City - Madison Square Garden
14-6-77	New York City - Madison Square Garden
19-6-77	San Diego - Sports Arena
21-6-77	Los Angeles - Forum
22-6-77	Los Angeles - Forum
23-6-77	Los Angeles - Forum (Keith Moon of The Who jams on encore)
25-6-77	Los Angeles - Forum
26-6-77	Los Angeles - Forum

27-6-77	Los Angeles - Forum
17-7-77	Seattle - Kingdome
20-7-77	Tempe - Activities Centre Arena
23-7-77	Oakland - Oakland Coliseum
24-7-77	Oakland - Oakland Coliseum
30-7-77	New Orleans - Superdrome (cancelled due to sudden death of Plant's son Karac)
2-8-77	Chicago - Chicago Stadium (cancelled)
3-8-77	Chicago - Chicago Stadium (cancelled)
6-8-77	Buffalo - Rich Stadium (cancelled)
9-8-77	Pittsburg - Arena (cancelled)
10-8-77	Pittsburg - Arena (cancelled)
13-8-77	Philadelphia - JFK Stadium (cancelled)

Warm-up shows

23-7-79	Copenhagen, Denmark - Falkonertheatre
24-7-79	Copenhagen, Denmark - Falkonertheatre

The UK return

4-8-79	Knebworth Festival
11-8-79	Knebworth Festival

Fourth European tour

17-6-80	Dortmund, Germany - Westfalenhalle
18-6-80	Cologne, Germany - Sporthalle
20-6-80	Brussels, Belgium - Vorst National
21-6-80	Rotterdam, Holland - Ahoy
23-6-80	Bremmen, Germany - Stadhalle
24-6-80	Hanover, Germany - Messenhalle
26-6-80	Vienna, Austria - Stadhalle
27-6-80	Nuremburg, Germany - Messezen

	trumhalle (show abandoned after 15 minutes due to Bonzo's illness)
29-6-80	Zurich, Switzerland - Hallenstadion
30-6-80	Frankfurt, Germany - Festhalle
2-7-80	Mannheim, Germany - Eisstadium
3-7-80	Mannheim, Germany - Eisstadium
5-7-80	Munich, Germany - Olympiahalle (Bad Co's Simon Kirke jams on encore)
7-7-80	Berlin, Germany - Eissporthalle (The final show)

*An asterisk denotes that there is some speculation as to whether these dates were played. It proved difficult to verify some of the more obscure dates.

Led Zeppelin and their management have never allowed public access to their official files.

This Concert Log has been compiled after several years of extensive research utilising numerous sources the National Music Press (concert reviews and adverts), local news agencies, photographers notes, posters, ticket stubs, live tapes and after many hours of conversations with associates of the band. For some tours, I also obtained access to official roadcrew itineraries, which proved to be invaluable references.

Simon Pallett 1993

Picture credits

The Publisher would like to thank the following for their kind permission to reproduce the photographs in this book:

Terri Berg/Neil Zlozower, 75, 121 bottom right, 125, 175 top left;

Jill Furmanovsky, 39 bottom, 40, 42 top left, 43, 44, 45, 46, 53, 54, 55, 56, 57, 59, 60-61, 81, 153, 162-3;

London Features International, 19, 20 top, 31 bottom, 32 left and right, 33, 37, 41, 47 top and right of centre, 48-9, 139 top, 164 top, 165, 169 top right, **Simon Fowler,** 139 bottom right, 145 centre, 146, 150, 151, 152, 175 centre, **Andy Kent,** 162 left; **Neal Preston,** 145 top right;

The Howard Mylett Collection, 10 top and bottom, 14 top left, 16 bottom left, 17 bottom right, 26 bottom left and right, 27, 36 bottom, 39, 42 bottom right, 77 top and bottom, 117, 161 bottom right, 170, 175, **Adrian Boot,**79; **Chris Brown,** 9 bottom; **Richard Brown,** 173 centre, **Chris Drela,** 8, 29; **Carl L Dunn,** back endpaper, 18, 23 top right, right of centre and bottom, 26 top left, 38, 64 bottom right, 65, 66-67 top, 67 bottom, 68 top right, 72 right of centre, 73, 74, 90, 92, 93, 95 left,102 top, 105 right of centre, 126, 163, 168 top left, 173, 174, 176; **Hipgnosis,** 131, 135, 137, 157, 158, 159, 164 bottom, 175 below centre; **Brian Knapp,** 129; **Lancashire Evening-Post,** 52 top; **Stewart Pearsall,** 160; **Alan Perry,**141 bottom

right;**Barry Plummer,** 91; **Joe Stevens,** 80; **Angelika Stitch-nothe,** 161 top left; **Nando Valverde,** 114; **Pictorial Press,** 20 bottom, 72 bottom left, 172, **Richard E Aaron/Star File,** 124 bottom right, **Bob Gruen/Star File,** 50-51, 123 centre, 128, 168, **Joe Sia/Star File,** 29 top, 31 top;

Barry Plummer, front endpaper, 21 bottom, 24-25, 25 top right, 28, 30, 94 top and bottom, 95 right, 9 bottom left, 102 bottom left, 107, 133, 143 bottom right, 140-141, 144, 167;

Redferns, 127 bottom, **Richie Aaron** 116 centre and bottom right, 120-121, 122, 124, **Dick Barnatt,** 6 left and right, 7 left and right, 15, 16 top, **Fin Costello,** 34, 35, **Ian Dickson,** 97 top right, 98-99, 103, 106, 169 bottom left, **Dave Ellis,** 64 top left, **David Redfern,** 68 bottom left, 69 top right, 148-9, 171;

Relay Photos, 11, 22, 36 top left, 96, **Richard Creamer,** 127 top right, **André Csilag,** 142-143 top, **Chris Walter,** 14 bottom right, 70 top, 123 top right;

Rex Features, 9 top, 12 left and right, 13, 17 top left, 21 top, 111 bottom, **Chris Foster,** 71;

Pennie Smith, 62, 63, 69 bottom, 70 bottom, 82-3, 84, 86, 88-89, 100, 101, 104, 105top left, 108, 109,111 top, 112, 113, 115, 118-9, 138, 147, 155.